Gambling

Other books in the Social Issues Firsthand series:

Adoption

Capital Punishment

Death and Dying

The Environment

Family Violence

Homosexuality

Interracial Relationships

Poverty

Prisons

Racism

Religion

Suicide

Terrorism

SOCIAL ISSUES
FIRSTHAND

Gambling

Jill Hamilton, Book Editor

GREENHAVEN PRESS

An imprint of Thomson Gale, a part of The Thomson Corporation

Detroit • New York • San Francisco • New Haven, Conn. • Waterville, Maine • London • Munich

Bonnie Szumski, *Publisher*
Helen Cothran, *Managing Editor*

© 2006 Thomson Gale, a part of The Thomson Corporation.

For more information, contact:
Greenhaven Press
27500 Drake Rd.
Farmington Hills, MI 48331-3535
Or you can visit our Internet site at http://www.gale.com

LIBRARY OF CONGRESS CATALOGING-IN-PUBLICATION DATA

Gambling / Jill Hamilton, book editor.
  p. cm. -- (Social issues firsthand)
  Includes bibliographical references and index.
  ISBN 0-7377-2498-6
  1. Gambling. 2. Gamblers. 3. Compulsive gamblers--Rehabilitation. 4. Casinos--Employees. I. Hamilton, Jill. II. Series.
  HV6710.G3142 2007
  363.4'2--dc22

                                                          2006043387

Printed in the United States of America
10 9 8 7 6 5 4 3 2 1

Contents

Foreword   **7**

Introduction   **10**

Chapter 1: Professional and Recreational Gamblers

1. A Poker Player's Life, Then and Now   **15**

   Josh Arieh

   A professional poker player describes how the game has changed in the past decade.

2. How I Became a Low Roller   **21**

   Jean Scott

   A woman describes how she and her husband became experts at getting free meals and hotel rooms from the casinos where they gambled.

3. An Actor's Passion for Poker   **31**

   James Woods, interviewed by Michael Caselli

   A well-known actor discusses his life as a celebrity poker player.

4. Confessions of an Underground Poker Junkie   **39**

   Alice H. Kim

   A female amateur poker player describes the growing card club scene in New York.

Chapter 2: The Struggles of Gambling Addicts

1. How I Was Snared by Online Gambling   **46**

   Maureen Paton

   A British woman turns to online gambling to cope with her father's death and becomes addicted to the games.

2. I Am a Lottery Ticket Addict   **51**

   Chris Wright

   A recovering gambling addict describes his addiction to scratch lottery tickets and his decision to quit playing the lottery.

3. I Am in Residential Treatment for My Gambling   **64**
David

A young resident of Gordon House, a treatment center for problem gamblers, discusses his descent into addiction.

4. My Brother Was a Compulsive Gambler   **68**
Michelle Wong

A Calgary filmmaker explores her brother's gambling addiction and suicide.

Chapter 3: Working at the Casino

1. A Day in the Life Behind the Tables   **75**
Jason DuVall

A casino employee describes a typical day working at the blackjack and roulette tables, meeting college kids, tourists, and drunken patrons.

2. The Dark Side of Casinos   **83**
Kim K.

A casino surveillance officer describes the activities she observes from behind the cameras in casino security.

3. Interview with a Blackjack Dealer   **90**
Sandy, interviewed by Robert Romano

"Sandy," a twenty-year casino veteran, discusses obnoxious customers, her financial situation, and cheaters.

Organizations to Contact   **96**

For Further Research   **100**

Index   **105**

Foreword

Social issues are often viewed in abstract terms. Pressing challenges such as poverty, homelessness, and addiction are viewed as problems to be defined and solved. Politicians, social scientists, and other experts engage in debates about the extent of the problems, their causes, and how best to remedy them. Often overlooked in these discussions is the human dimension of the issue. Behind every policy debate over poverty, homelessness, and substance abuse, for example, are real people struggling to make ends meet, to survive life on the streets, and to overcome addiction to drugs and alcohol. Their stories are ubiquitous and compelling. They are the stories of everyday people—perhaps your own family members or friends—and yet they rarely influence the debates taking place in state capitols, the national Congress, or the courts.

The disparity between the public debate and private experience of social issues is well illustrated by looking at the topic of poverty. Each year the U.S. Census Bureau establishes a poverty threshold. A household with an income below the threshold is defined as poor, while a household with an income above the threshold is considered able to live on a basic subsistence level. For example, in 2003 a family of two was considered poor if its income was less than $12,015; a family of four was defined as poor if its income was less than $18,810. Based on this system, the bureau estimates that 35.9 million Americans (12.5 percent of the population) lived below the poverty line in 2003, including 12.9 million children below the age of eighteen.

Commentators disagree about what these statistics mean. Social activists insist that the huge number of officially poor Americans translates into human suffering. Even many families that have incomes above the threshold, they maintain, are likely to be struggling to get by. Other commentators insist that the statistics exaggerate the problem of poverty in the United States. Compared to people in developing countries, they point out, most so-called poor families have a high quality of life. As stated by journalist Fidelis Iyebote, "Cars are owned by 70 percent of 'poor' households. . . . Color televisions belong to 97 percent of the 'poor' [and] videocassette recorders belong to nearly 75 percent. . . . Sixty-four percent have microwave ovens, half own a stereo system, and over a quarter possess an automatic dishwasher."

However, this debate over the poverty threshold and what it means is likely irrelevant to a person living in poverty. Simply put, poor people do not need the government to tell them whether they are poor. They can see it in the stack of bills they cannot pay. They are aware of it when they are forced to choose between paying rent or buying food for their children. They become painfully conscious of it when they lose their homes and are forced to live in their cars or on the streets. Indeed, the written stories of poor people define the meaning of poverty more vividly than a government bureaucracy could ever hope to. Narratives composed by the poor describe losing jobs due to injury or mental illness, depict horrific tales of childhood abuse and spousal violence, recount the loss of friends and family members. They evoke the slipping away of social supports and government assistance, the descent into substance abuse and addiction, the harsh realities of life on the streets. These are the perspectives on poverty that are too often omitted from discussions over the extent of the problem and how to solve it.

Greenhaven Press's Social Issues Firsthand series provides a forum for the often-overlooked human perspectives on society's most divisive topics of debate. Each volume focuses on one social issue and presents a collection of ten to sixteen narratives by those who have had personal involvement with the topic. Extra care has been taken to include a diverse range of perspectives. For example, in the volume on adoption, readers will find the stories of birth parents who have made an adoption plan, adoptive parents, and adoptees themselves. After exposure to these varied points of view, the reader will have a clearer understanding that adoption is an intense, emotional experience full of joyous highs and painful lows for all concerned.

The debate surrounding embryonic stem cell research illustrates the moral and ethical pressure that the public brings to bear on the scientific community. However, while nonexperts often criticize scientists for not considering the potential negative impact of their work, ironically the public's reaction against such discoveries can produce harmful results as well. For example, although the outcry against embryonic stem cell research in the United States has resulted in fewer embryos being destroyed, those with Parkinson's, such as actor Michael J. Fox, have argued that prohibiting the development of new stem cell lines ultimately will prevent a timely cure for the disease that is killing Fox and thousands of others.

Each book in the series contains several features that enhance its usefulness, including an in-depth introduction, an annotated table of contents, bibliographies for further research, a list of organizations to contact, and a thorough index. These elements—combined with the poignant voices of people touched by tragedy and triumph—make the Social Issues Firsthand series a valuable resource for research on today's topics of political discussion.

Introduction

Gambling was once associated with gangsters or shady poker games in a back room, but now it has a new image. Instead of outlawing or condemning gambling, the government and many religious organizations are often the ones running the games. State laws against gambling have been replaced by state-run lotteries, and many churches now hold casino nights to raise money for charity. Today, forty-eight states have some form of legalized gambling. Las Vegas, which was once seen as an edgy "Sin City," is now touted as a family-friendly vacation destination. Gambling is one of America's fastest growing industries and has become more popular than baseball or movies. However, as gambling has become more socially acceptable, the rate of gambling addiction has soared.

One of the factors contributing to the growing number of gambling addicts is the ever increasing availability of gambling venues. At one time, people had to travel to Las Vegas or Atlantic City, New Jersey, to gamble, but now casinos have sprouted up all over the country, and for many, gambling opportunities are only a short drive away. Whereas in the past, potentially out-of-control gamblers were only able to indulge their habit with an occasional vacation to a casino town, the convenience of nearby casinos has allowed many to develop a dangerous addiction. According to a report in the *Harvard Mental Health Letter*, among people who live within fifty miles of a casino, the percentage of compulsive gamblers is about twice the national average.

The Rise of Online Gambling

The advent of Internet gambling (or "gaming," as gambling proponents like to call it) in 1995 has also made it easier to become a problem gambler. Now people wishing to gamble not only do not have to go to Las Vegas, they do not even have to get out of their pajamas. Each month more than 1.8 million computer users play online poker, and many of these gamblers become addicted. According to a 2002 University of Connecticut study, at least 74 percent of online gamblers have a serious gambling problem.

Some people who begin gambling as a casual hobby become addicted to online games. "Whenever I hit a jackpot, a message kept flashing: 'Play for real! You could win real money!'" says Lisa Harding, a thirty-nine-year-old mother of two who at first played games online only for fun. "So I started betting with my credit card."[1] She and her husband Andy soon had online gambling debts of over one hundred thousand dollars.

Online gambling makes it easy for addicts to gamble secretly. People can gamble twenty-four hours a day, and if no one sees them doing it, no one is going to suggest that they take a break or recognize that they have a problem. "I played for twelve, fifteen hours straight, wouldn't do anything but gamble,"[2] reports "Alex," an Indiana University junior who lost fifty-five thousand dollars playing online. Money spent online also can seem less real to players. "If I lose a ton of money, it's not that big a deal. It's like a video game,"[3] says Vanessa Selbst, a college student who plays online poker.

The Growing Number of Gambling Addicts

As gambling has become more accessible, the profile of the problem gambler has changed to include both teenagers and senior citizens. "The two huge areas now are youth and senior gambling,"[4] states Richard L., a member of Gamblers Anonymous in Tacoma, Washington. According to the National Council on Problem Gambling, more than 70 percent of young people between ten and seventeen years old have gambled in the past year, up 45 percent from 1988. There are several reasons for the increase. First, people have more opportunities to gamble than they did in the past, when gambling required sneaking into a casino or finding a secret poker game. Now anyone with access to a credit card can be online and gambling in minutes. In addition, gambling has become a well-publicized fad. Celebrities publicly profess their love of poker, and TV stations broadcast poker games, creating celebrities in a pastime that previously did not receive much publicity.

Young people are gambling more; they are starting at an earlier age, and they are playing for higher stakes. This puts them at a great risk. Research has found that people who start gambling as children or teenagers are three times more likely to develop a gambling problem than people who begin gambling as adults. As Keith Whyte, an executive of the National Council on Problem Gambling, notes, "The earlier you start gambling, the more likely you will be to have a gambling problem."[5]

Gambling has also become a problem for many senior citizens, who are particularly vulnerable for several reasons. They may turn to gambling in order to fill too much free time, to cope with the death of loved ones, to try to supplement a meager income, or simply to spend time with other people. Seniors are also a favorite target group for casinos, which advertise heavily to that age group, offering bargains such as free or low-cost transportation to casinos.

Coping with Gambling Addiction

Gambling addiction is a particularly difficult problem. For people with a gambling problem, gambling is as potent as any drug. In order to support their habit some gamblers end up neglecting their jobs or schoolwork, stealing from their employers or loved ones to gamble or to pay off gambling debts, and ruining relationships. Once people have become addicted to the momentary high of winning money, they will continue to gamble to attempt to recapture the feeling of a previous win. Even when problem gamblers lose a lot of money and get into overwhelming financial trouble, they continue to believe that their next game or gamble will be the "big win" that will allow them to recoup their losses.

The treatments for problem gambling are like those for other addictive behaviors. One of the most popular ways to seek help is to join a group support program such as Gamblers Anonymous, which is based on principles similar to Alcoholics Anonymous. In addition, the National Council on Problem Gambling offers a twenty-four-hour confidential hotline for people concerned about their own gambling or the gambling habits of someone they know. Problem gamblers can also seek help from specially trained counselors or residential treatment programs. Researchers are currently investigating the use of antidepressants as a treatment for gambling addiction, but the results are still inconclusive.

Gambling is a major social issue that affects millions of people around the world. In *Social Issues Firsthand: Gambling*, the authors provide personal narratives about their own experiences with gambling as well as stories about family members who gamble. These experiences range from positive to devastating. For some of the essayists, gambling is a social diversion or a mental challenge, while for others, it is an out-of-control addiction. For the employees of casinos, gambling offers an interesting way to make a living. The account of each author in this volume provides a human perspective on a social issue that provokes much debate among scholars, politicians, and others concerned about the role of gambling in people's lives.

Notes

1. Quoted in Alex Tresniowski, "Gambling Online," *People*, October 13, 2003.
2. Quoted in Daniel G. Habib, "Online and Obsessed," *Sports Illustrated*, May 30, 2005.
3. Quoted in Habib, "Online and Obsessed."
4. Quoted in Marsha King, "Gambling Addiction on the Rise Among Seniors," *Seattle Times*, November 23, 2005.
5. Quoted in Alexandra Marks, "Youth Gamblers on the Rise," *Christian Science Monitor*, March 25, 2005.

CHAPTER 1

Professional and Recreational Gamblers

A Poker Player's Life, Then and Now

Josh Arieh

Josh Arieh is a professional poker player with more than fourteen years' experience playing the game. He has won two World Series of Poker championships and appears often on televised poker games. In the following selection Arieh compares his not so distant past of playing poker with novices in pool halls and cheap hotel rooms with his experiences playing professional poker in world class tournaments. Arieh recalls that when he first decided to become a professional gambler he preferred to tell people he was self-employed because most reacted negatively when he told them he was a professional card player. Arieh writes about the changes brought about by the World Series of Poker Tour and how peoples' attitudes and perceptions of professional poker players have changed dramatically since the mid-1990s, so that now many professional poker players are celebrities and many celebrities have ambitions of becoming high-stakes poker players. Arieh also explains some of the logistics of televised poker and the difficulties of playing on camera.

It's 2 A.M. on a Friday night, sometime in the mid Nineties. All the desperate gamblers flock to the poolroom with high hopes of doubling their modest bankrolls. Fireworks are going off in my head, knowing that, within hours, I will have all these guys crowded around a small coffee table at the nearest hotel, playing my game—poker. On any given night, we would have a caravan of five to ten cars leave the poolroom parking lot, and flow into the closest Motel 6. I was the leader of the pack; I didn't mind paying for a hotel room to play in, because I knew that by the end of the night all the money would be in my pocket.

Josh Arieh, "Then and Now," *Bluff*, December-January 2004. Reproduced by permission.

Ten years ago, the games of choice were Omaha Hi/Lo and Limit Hold'em. Boy, how times have changed. I started out playing in back-room pool halls and $30-a-night hotel rooms. Now we are playing in plush casinos, with television cameras peeking down on us from every angle. In the old days, you could mumble something under your breath and not worry about anyone hearing it. Now I have a wireless 'mic' begging me to say something controversial.

My opponents? Well, they used to be novices. I used to get my rush from busting players with names like 'Jer Jer' and '8-ball Paul'. Nowadays I'm getting check-raised by the likes of Phil Ivey and Daniel Negreanu, and I'd be the first to say there's no fun in that.

First World Series of Poker Tournament

It's easy for me look back and visualize the beginning of my professional poker career in early 1999. Once I realized that being a courier wasn't my life's ambition, I quit to pursue something else; although I wasn't sure exactly what that would be. I was playing poker part-time, picking up a little money here and there, when a friend of mine, Mark Wilds, asked me to come out to the WSOP [World Series of Poker] to play a few events. In the preceding few months I had been playing a lot of heads-up poker, and Mark thought it would be great tournament experience.

I was young, wet behind the ears, and didn't know what failure was. No matter what I did, I expected to win. If I was sitting across from Johnny Chan or Phil Helmuth, it didn't matter; I was going to find a way to win. My first tournament was a disaster. I was too naive to realize that an all-nighter and a round of golf beforehand was not the right preparation for a world-class event. After one of my patented sixteen-hour power sessions of sleep, I was ready to get back in the box when the $3000 Limit Hold'em tournament kicked off. After a grueling day of playing, I made the final table and was in fourth chip position.

If I knew then what I know now, there is no way I would have won that tournament. I hadn't a clue who Howard Lederer, John Juanda, Tom Franklin, Humburto Brenes, and Jack Fox were. They were just players at the table, and to this day I have no idea how I won. I've always said that the stars must have lined up perfectly that day, for me to overcome that level of competition in one of my first major events.

I look back at that tournament as the beginning of my career. The days of flying below the radar were over; the days of picking off the boys at the poolroom were no more. It was time to say goodbye to 'Jer Jer' and '8-ball Paul'. I was still the same person; I just had more money and a whole bunch more 'gamble'.

Changes in the World of Poker

As the years flew past, you could see the face of poker changing. Many more young people were becoming attracted to the game, and that was when the television companies started getting involved. The World Poker Tour was born—and it was about to change poker, as we knew it, forever. Poker players were no longer looked down upon; on the contrary, we were placed right in the limelight like never before.

You have to remember the history of poker. It was played in the backs of bars and poolrooms, and, until recently, had been booted out of most of the nation's casinos and replaced by highdollar slot machines. I remember clearly telling people what I did for a living and seeing their reactions; I was little better than a convict. I can't tell you how many times I heard: "Isn't that illegal in Georgia?" and I must say it grew old fast. It got to the point that my wife was telling people I was 'self–

Carlos Mortensen of Spain celebrates his $1.5 million win at the 2001 World Series of Poker, played at Binion's Horseshoe Hotel and Casino in Las Vegas, Nevada. In 2005, the World Series winner received a record $7.5 million. © Reuters/Corbis.

employed' and leaving it at that. Nowadays, the only time I tell people I'm a professional poker player is when I have half an hour to spare, because Joe Public is infatuated with the game, and wants to know every last detail.

Don't get me wrong. I love the attention, and I'm extremely grateful to the people who have helped poker to grow. Less than two years ago, third place in the WSOP was worth less than $500k, and this year my third-place finish won me a whopping $2.5 million. Every poker player should be grateful to two people in particular for getting poker noticed by the mainstream: Steve Lipscomb, the brains behind getting the WPT on television, and Chris Moneymaker. After Chris won the WSOP, the number of entrants skyrocketed from in the mid-800's to over two and a half thousand.

Playing on Camera

I have been fortunate enough to experience 'TV poker' from the inside of both major venues. My first experience was the last few days of the WSOP, which I must say was the time of my life. I was able to play at the biggest table in the history of poker and show the world my skills. Had Lady Luck swapped a few cards here and there, it could have easily been me, the World Champion of Poker! Man, that's got a nice little ring to it. Although, that's not taking anything away from Greg Raymer; he played magnificently throughout, is a great guy, and the perfect player to represent poker as our World Champion.

The WSOP television coverage setup was excellent. For those of you unfamiliar with the routine, "Lemme tell ya!" Each of the nine spots at the final table has a lipstick camera in the railing with a small dot in front of it. Before you sit down to play, you are instructed to look at your hole cards over that dot so the camera can see your cards. I played hundreds of hands at that table, and was only once told to show my hole cards to the camera more clearly.

Recently, I finished third in the WPT [World Poker Tour] event at the Borgata, and it seemed like every other hand they were asking me to show my hole cards to the camera again. That really screwed up my rhythm. I'm used to dim pool halls and hotel rooms with one lap, not game-show sets with cameras behind me. Maybe next time I'll be better prepared for the WPT thing and know what to expect. I understand that they have a show to put on, but the gameflow should be the priority, not the production mumbo jumbo. So here is a bit of advice for someone that is going to a TV table: poker is not what it used to be.

When the big money is on the line, it's going to be hard to get into your normal comfort zone, like you would at your local home game, or if you were coming down the stretch of one of these internet tournaments. Before the hand-play starts, get comfortable, take in all the sights and get ready for bright lights, smoke effects and announcers. Don't act like I did, thinking you're fine and you can get comfortable in any environment. It's like preparing yourself for a big road-game in hostile territory.

How I Became a Low Roller

Jean Scott

Jean Scott's evangelical fundamentalist minister father was so opposed to gambling that his children were not allowed to play any games with dice. As Scott describes in the next selection, she did not learn the real names for card suits until she was in her thirties. To her, a club was a "clover." Her first experience gambling was playing gin rummy for a penny a point with a close friend. Scott writes that she enjoyed playing cards and in 1984 took her first trip to Las Vegas with her husband. They started playing slot machines and low-stakes blackjack but quickly became high rollers, spending $3,000 to $4,000 on three-day trips. When the expense and sleep deprivation of their quick trips started to wear on them, they tried to find a different way to enjoy gambling. They discovered that they could become "low rollers" by playing cheaper games like video poker, which extended their gambling time and cost less money. The Scotts found that by taking advantage of the "comps," or freebies, offered by casinos, they could extend their trips into weeks or months, all while enjoying free drinks, hotel rooms, and meals.

Playing games has always been in my blood. One of my earliest memories is sitting cross-legged on the floor playing Uncle Wiggley. I was three or four years old, still an only child. I'd pester my mother, "Please play a game with me." She was often at the ironing board or sewing machine and too busy to participate, but she'd say, "OK, honey, I'll play. You set it up."

I'd pull out the Uncle Wiggley board and twirl the spinner and take my turn—hop hop hop—moving the number of spaces the spinner indicated. Then I'd say, "It's your turn,

Mother," and she'd say, "You spin for me." So I'd spin for her and move her game piece. Even though I was doing all the work, it didn't matter; I was playing a game and I was happy.

To this day I remember the intense feeling of competitiveness I had as a child. Even at age four and five, sitting at a Chutes and Ladders board, I played to win. It was a very important, even passionate, part of my life.

It may seem like a long way from a kiddie board game on a threadbare rug in a simple Pennsylvania home to dollar deuces wild and the luxurious hotel rooms, free meals, and first-class entertainment given to us by palace-like casinos all over the world. Yet the spirit is exactly the same—intense, competitive, playing to win.

Growing Up as a Preacher's Kid

Where I am today is even more remarkable considering where I was back then. My father is an evangelical fundamentalist minister, so I was a "PK," a preacher's kid. We had no cards or dice in our home. If a game that we wanted to play came with dice, we'd have to throw them away and use a spinner from one of our other kiddie games instead. Cards and dice were symbols of gambling, which was very much against our religion. But our family always played games. From the simple don't-have-to-read-the-rules games, I graduated to Chinese checkers, chess, and finally Monopoly, the ultimate of all board games, I thought.

Many first-born children are resentful of their younger siblings, but not I! I was exceedingly grateful when my parents provided me with two sisters with whom to play games. My parents were grateful too, because now I didn't pester them to play with me all the time. My family played games almost every night except Wednesdays (which was prayer-meeting night); on Sundays we played religious games. My mother would cook up a big bowl of popcorn and we'd pull out a board game. When we three girls were old enough to play

Scrabble, the family's competitiveness really blossomed. My father is 83, and to this day one of his greatest pleasures in life is to get together with his three girls, play Scrabble, and beat all three of us. Even though he oversaw a very strict and religious household, the gaming spirit was strong.

Because we were not allowed to have playing cards in the house, I didn't learn the four suits until I was in my early thirties. We weren't even allowed to play games like Old Maid, because that would have had the appearance of sinful behavior. Someone might have seen us playing and thought we were engaged in a poker game! When I got married, I finally started to play cards, but not "real" card games. We went through a period of Old Maid, Rook, and Pit, just enough to broaden my life a little bit.

Learning the Suits

When I was thirty-five, things changed: I left the fundamentalist environment and embarked on a new kind of life. That's when I finally decided it was okay to play games like gin rummy and poker, so I had to learn the suits. Even today, sometimes I still think of a club as a "clover" or a spade as a "digger," because that's the way I learned them. At that time I had a close friend who played a lot of cards. He taught me how to play gin rummy. I took to it immediately. We played for a penny a point and for years we kept a running total in a notebook; since he'd been playing all his life, I wound up owing him quite a lot of pennies. Luckily, he became my second husband so I never had to pay off! But this was my first experience playing a game for money, not just for the pleasurable feeling of competition and trying to win. Even though it was only pennies (that would never be paid), suddenly I realized that playing for real money added a whole new spice to the gaming experience that I had never known before.

Next came Tonk and Euchre, card games that are extremely popular in the Midwest. Both are played for money and my husband and I played them around the kitchen table with our friends, again just for small stakes. Then I started driving 30 miles to where my husband worked so I could play Tonk with him and his co-workers on their lunch hour. They played for dollars, and that's when my competitive spirit finally roared up from deep inside me like a geyser. I took to the higher stakes very quickly. I became an excellent Tonk player and found myself beating others who'd played a lot longer than I had. It was only then, several decades after Uncle Wiggley, that I realized I was a natural at gambling.

Eventually, my husband and I joined a Moose Lodge where there was a Tonk game from ten in the morning till midnight almost every day of the week. Whenever I had a spare hour or two from raising my children or teaching high school English, that's where I would be. The stakes were quite a bit higher; therefore, the challenge and pleasure were greater.

Starting as High Rollers

I took my first trip to Las Vegas in 1984. Although I'd been playing cards for only a few years, my husband Brad had been gambling since he was five (he had two older brothers as teachers). But neither of us knew a thing about casino gambling, so we played the no-brainer slot machines and a little seat-of-the-pants low-stakes blackjack. We lost our entire gambling bankroll, but we enjoyed that trip so much that we knew we would return to Vegas as often as we could.

Hoping to improve our results, we attended a blackjack seminar in our hometown and learned basic strategy. Then we went to the library and put ourselves through a crash course on card counting. We practiced and practiced and practiced—and got good enough to raise the stakes considerably.

It's funny to think of it now, but we began our casino careers as high rollers. We bet green ($25) and black ($100) chips, and went on junkets to Las Vegas, Reno-Tahoe, and Atlantic City, sometimes on private casino airplanes. We ate in all the gourmet restaurants, saw the best shows, and had the most luxurious rooms. We were living the good life. Then we broadened our horizons and went on junkets to San Juan, Santo Domingo, even Monaco. That was the ultimate junket. Our airfare was paid, we stopped in Paris for four days, and then it was on to Monte Carlo, where everything was comped, even at the exorbitant European prices.

Looking back on that era, I feel we did fairly well for ourselves. We lost more money than we won, because we weren't the greatest card counters, but we made more than enough in comps to cover our losses. It was pretty heady living in the rarefied air of the high roller.

Retiring to Vegas

Then in 1989, Brad retired and we decided that we wanted to spend more of our time in casino locations. That's when we started to consider a different lifestyle. We began to think that the way we were doing it—taking $3,000–$4,000 and flying to Tahoe for three or four days—was too hectic. Those few days just weren't long enough: we gambled too long, we didn't get enough sleep, and we didn't have enough time to enjoy all the "real-life" things that beckoned to us from outside the casino. Also, on occasion we'd lose a good portion of our gambling bankroll, and it all seemed too fleeting, too transitory, for the price we were paying.

So we decided to take the $3,000 or $4,000 and try to make it last longer—a lot longer—three or four weeks instead of three or four days. We knew that the best place to do it was Las Vegas, with its proliferation of competing casinos. We decided to trade the first-class short-term treatment for less luxurious amenities over a longer period of time and, in the process, reduce our gambling risk. Besides, about that time the casinos were starting to cut down considerably on what they were giving back in comps to table players; you had to bet more and more to get the good stuff. So we reduced our bets to red chips ($5) and spent a couple of years doing quite well working the lower end of the scale.

We now went to Las Vegas for a week, two weeks, three weeks at a time. We weren't staying at the higher-class hotels like Caesar's Palace, but at older casinos like the Riviera, Holiday Inn (now Harrah's), and the Westward Ho. We learned how to work the comp system and discovered that we didn't miss the gourmet meals (even when it's free, fancy food isn't good for the waistline or the cholesterol count). Playing $5 and $10 blackjack, we could still get comps for all the food we could eat—at good buffets and coffee shops. We could also get our rooms at the discounted "casino rate" (typically 40%–50% off the rack rate). Occasionally, our combined blackjack action would earn us a free night or two.

Life as a Low Roller

As time went by, I began to notice that Brad would be gone from the blackjack tables (while we were playing and being rated) for longer and longer periods. I wondered where he went, afraid the pit bosses would get after him for staying away from the table—just leaving his chips and disappearing. We already knew that you should leave the table as often as possible, because you were being rated by the hour and as long as you left your chips at the game, the comp clock kept ticking. Finally, he confessed that he was running over to the machines and playing video poker.

I thought, "Oh no, *not* video poker!" Everyone knows slot machine players are uninformed and can't win. I figured only a real loser would go from blackjack to video poker. Brad, on the other hand, looked at things differently. "But, Jean, I'm only putting in quarters and I'm not losing that much," he insisted. "Besides, it's so relaxing and fun."

And he was right. Blackjack gets tiring, particularly when you're counting cards. We couldn't play for long periods at a time, so following Brad's lead, I decided to take a (skeptical) look. When we left the tables and stopped the comp clock, I'd sit at the video poker machines, watching while he tried his luck.

Then in January 1990 we were playing at the Stardust when I noticed advertisements about a "slot club." When I investigated, I found that it didn't cost anything to join and members got comps, prizes, even cash back, for their play. I said to Brad, "As long as you're gonna be putting money into these machines, we might as well get something back for it."

I started reading articles in various gambling magazines which claimed that video poker was a game of skill and that the payback could be very good, almost 100%. We also found that at the end of our trips, the Stardust would give us back $40–$50, based solely on Brad's video poker play. Better yet, when we went home, we started getting mail from the Stardust—invitations for free nights and meals and parties—which reminded us of when we were high rollers.

The next time we went to Las Vegas, we took advantage of the free nights at the Stardust and we started joining every slot club we could. Brad and I use different surnames, so we opened up two separate accounts at each casino, and I started playing video poker, too. Also, we studied up on the optimal strategy for 9/6 jacks or better video poker, so although we weren't winning, we weren't losing much while the comps continued to roll in.

We started to get lots of our nights comped, and since we were retired and had all the time in the world, we didn't mind moving around a bit to take advantage of as many offers as we could at the different casinos where we were slot club VIPs. A casino would send me an offer in the mail for three free nights, and Brad would get the same offer on the same day in the same mailbox. By combining our six nights at casino A, then accepting an offer for four nights between us at casino B, as well as another four nights at casino C, we all of a sudden were staying in Las Vegas for 14 nights, without paying for a single one! In addition to this, any time we asked, we got our food comped.

Settling In at the Video Poker Machines

To top it all off, we discovered that video poker was far more enjoyable than blackjack. Playing 21 is hard. Card counting requires constant mental calculations. First you have to calculate the true count, then divide by the number of decks remaining to derive the running count, then figure out how much to bet. All the while you worry that the pit boss is on to you as a counter and—horror of horrors!—you'll get thrown out of the casino and have to start all over again somewhere else. I'd already been barred from one casino in Tahoe for counting cards, so these fears were genuine. And for me, there was a more pressing problem. I'd always played a good game of blackjack with basic strategy, but when I counted cards, I think my lips moved slightly. I was an English teacher and math never came easily to me, so when I counted, I had to do it almost verbally. It was exhausting!

But playing video poker, we could sit side by side at the machines and laugh and drink diet soda and not worry about a thing. We knew the jacks or better strategy so well that we barely had to think about it, and we were getting the same comps that we did playing $5 and $10 blackjack. It was all so much more fun.

Before long, we started noticing deuces wild video poker machines and began talking to people who were playing them. We quickly learned that unlike jacks or better, the deuces wild variation was a positive game (meaning it paid back more than 100%). We went to Gamblers Book Club, paid $9.95 for a booklet on video poker in Las Vegas (by Lenny Frome), and studied the strategy for deuces.

The first time we sat down in front of a deuces wild machine was New Year's Eve 1991. I held the book while Brad played, and every time a hand popped up that we weren't sure how to play, I looked it up on the chart. After a couple of hours of playing, I had a headache from all the smoke and noise and retired to the room, leaving the strategy book with Brad. About an hour later the phone rang. It was Brad. "Guess what? I just hit the $1,000 royal flush!" I laughed, "Well, I guess that pays for our $9.95 strategy book!"

The Queen of Comps

Soon it was smooth sailing. The comps kept rolling in, we learned to take advantage of promotions, we perfected the strategies for many of the video poker variations, and we were having a blast. We'd gone from $100 bets to $5 bets at blackjack, then to $1.25 a hand at video poker. We were getting more comps and freebies from the casinos playing $1.25 video poker than we ever did playing $100 blackjack. Our transition from high rollers to low rollers was complete.

For us, making the most of the low-roller system (initially) culminated in December–January 1993. During those two months we played no blackjack at all (except during special promotions). Instead, we sat at the video poker machines. This was the longest Las Vegas trip we had undertaken. We stayed for 50 days, including Christmas, New Years, and the Super Bowl. We paid for a room on only one night. (We could've gotten that night free too, but we didn't want to bother switching hotel rooms for a single night.) The only meals we paid for were those we ate outside of the hotel-casinos when we just couldn't face another free buffet or coffee shop (poor us!). And because we managed to hit five royal flush jackpots, at the end of those 50 days we went home with $1,500 more than we left with.

It was for those feats that the *Las Vegas Advisor*, the famous consumer's newsletter for Las Vegas visitors, pegged me the "'Queen of Ku Pon,' the ruling monarch of the mythical magical kingdom of Low Roller." And two years later, when CBS's news magazine "48 Hours" did an entire show on gambling, two segments were devoted to Brad and me and our money-saving exploits. While introducing our story, [news anchor] Dan Rather gave me the title that has stuck: the "Queen of Comps."

An Actor's Passion for Poker

James Woods, interviewed by Michael Caselli

James Woods has been an actor since 1970 and is well known for his acclaimed performances in films like Salvador. *He has also joined the increasingly ubiquitous ranks of poker-playing celebrities. In the following interview with Michael Caselli, Woods describes his love of poker and poker players as well as the popularity of the game among other Hollywood stars, including actors Ben Affleck and Toby Maguire. Woods notes that he likes the mathematical challenge of poker but also enjoys the social aspects of the game. Woods also discusses his role in developing a poker Web site on which fans will be able to play with a variety of celebrities.*

Known for his intelligent, edgy performances, James Woods is now bringing the studied intensity of his film roles to the poker table. When *Bluff* [magazine] caught up with him, we actually managed to interrupt his morning online session, but, nevertheless, he was happy to wax lyrical to us about poker: his latest passionate obsession.

Excuse the interruption. You've been playing online?

Yes. Every morning I get up and think: 'Ok, while I'm reading the paper I'm gonna just play.' But there's a big distinction between playing and really playing—you get people who say—ok I'm gonna settle into the evening and play poker all night, and of course, what happens is they go up a bit, down a bit, you might have a little rush and then go back down, but by and large they're gonna kind of grind themselves down. What grinds you down more than anything else is fatigue—sheer fatigue.

Michael Caselli, "James Woods on Poker," *Bluff*, vol. 1, October-November 2004, pp. 46–47. Reproduced by permission.

A friend of mine, who was once in a terrible car accident, plays poker for a living—he hangs out at Hustler. He has to live off his poker winnings and plays incredibly tightly and aggressively—he plays the tightest hand imaginable, but when he's got it he plays. He will lay down a full house, if he thinks it might be the weaker full house, without even thinking about it; and the reason is he has to make five hundred dollars a day to live. He says: 'If I make five hundred, I take my five hundred and I get out of there before I make any mistakes.' He says you have to learn to be disciplined more than anything you could possibly imagine. So I thought: 'Well, I'm gonna try this as an experiment.'

So about five or six weeks ago, I decided to get up every morning and play, and I have a kind of ritual: I play with the dog a little bit and, before I take a shower, I order my room service (I'm in a hotel at the moment), read the paper and play online. Which means that I'm not enjoying myself (although I always do enjoy poker), but I'm gonna be playing just to win five hundred dollars, no more. That's my deal. The second I win five hundred, I log off.

The first month, I lost one day out of thirty-one days—so I've won every single day by playing incredibly, incredibly tight, not playing for fun. It's amazing what happens if you don't get emotionally involved in the game and you sit down to win.

Live Versus Online Play

Is it easier to play online that way than in a terrestrial tournament where things are more likely to get heated?

My biggest problem in live games is that I love the game so much and I don't think I ever met a poker player I didn't fundamentally like—even if they're screaming and they're acting like real jerks. I just love poker players. It's a great battle, and it really is a battle, and there are people from all walks of life, you know, never judge anybody at the table: a man can be the greatest poker player and he might know all the numbers, but he might get beaten by a really savvy kid who works in a grocery store; and that's what so great about this game. Because of who I am when I sit at a poker table I meet people who engage me in conversation, not only about poker, but also about the movie business and about the world of celebrities. The poker set don't really care that much about the Hollywood gossip—I've never heard Paris Hilton's name mentioned at a poker table. They're more like—I love that movie where ... and start talking about the movies, which can be a little distracting too.

You've starred in the movies "Casino" and "The Gambler"—is that what turned you on to gambling?

I'll tell you a great story that I haven't told many people. When I was a kid, about five or six years old, my dad, who was in the Korean War, had just gotten back and I was living with my mother. We were living with my father's mother in Illinois. My mother and her mother-in-law got along extraordinarily well—they loved each other—unlike most mother-in-law/daughter situations.

One thing we used to like to do together, believe it or not, was go to the bookies. You used to go up to this door in this alleyway, knock on the door with a certain number of knocks, and one of those little sliding things would open and they'd say: 'who sent you', and we'd say: 'Sam from the Candy Kitchen' because there was Sam's Candy Kitchen on the corner of our street. We were in this wonderful little town, it was just an amazingly wonderful place to grow up—so we'd go to the bookies, and it was like [the movie] *The Sting*—they'd be writing results from the race track on the blackboard; there'd be a guy on the telephone and people betting on the horses. And we went in once and the cops raided the place and my grandmother grabbed me—I was 5 or 5 1/2, and took me down the fire escape. My uncles got arrested but my mom and my grandmother and I got away—so I guess gambling's in my blood—although I never think of poker as gambling.

In fact I'll tell you how I got really interested in Texas Hold'em. A year ago this August [2004], I was with a friend of mine in Vegas and we were playing double bonus video poker, where you actually had a slight advantage, and, according to the Nevada gaming regulations, you had to pay out according to the specified percentages. But I noticed after 9/11 that the video poker machines just weren't streaking. It was just a gambler's feeling, but I got to talking to one of the slot hosts and he mentioned something about a new chip. I said, come on, don't bullshit me, what's going on. He said nothing and shrugged it off. So I got into my detective instincts and got talking to one of the tech guys and I said: 'So how is that new chip in the video poker machines?' and he said: 'You mean the new yield management chip?' and I say: 'Yeah that's the one, the yield management chip. What's the deal there?' And he said that after 9/11 the casinos were suffering and they petitioned the Nevada State Gaming Commission and asked them if they could still pay the same percentages, but defer the streaks by like a million hands.

They're so g—n f—in' greedy, they won't even let you enjoy the experience! And I said to my friend: 'I'm a smart guy, why am I sitting here in a completely and utterly losing situation and continuing to play? It's idiocy. I'm not going to do it any more and I love to gamble.' He said: 'You know what? You need to take up Texas Hold 'em.' I said: 'Why is that?' He said: 'Well, it's very simple to play, but the betting strategies are extraordinarily complex. You have a really good psychological mind. You went to MIT [Massachusetts Institute of Technology], majored in math and political science and minored in psychology—you have to have a good card sense and a good gambling instinct.' So I thought: 'Well, I'm gonna give it a try.' Well, the first time I played I won and I said, 'Oh, this is pretty good,' and I've played probably virtually every day since—online, at the casinos; and I read the books—everyday I reread, reread, reread, reread—If I'm waiting for a doctors' appointment, or in my car stuck in traffic or something—I pull over to the side and I just read a chapter; I reread until the other stuff is second nature—then you always read something that you read once and forgot about. Always.

The Hollywood Poker Craze

Why is poker seeping through Hollywood? It seems like everyone in the movies plays poker. . . .

Poker is really cool. Poker is where the action is these days and Hollywood is always in the center of the action. The reason why I'm involved in the opening HollywoodPoker.com, along with Vince Van Patten, the co-host of The World Poker Tour, is because we'd love to have a website where we can all play and enjoy the company of, not only other celebrities, but the poker players that I am interested in playing with. It's a kind of wonderful mix when you get celebrities interacting with their public. It usually happens at an event where—and I think this is sort of shameless—you have a big movie premier and you're walking down a red carpet, and the poor fans are stuck behind a velvet rope. I always make an extra effort to go and sign autographs—I like interacting with my fans. So I thought, hey, here's a website where I can interact with my fans and at the same time play, and hopefully beat, all my celebrity friends. And we get to play with the people who pay our salaries—and probably get beaten by them—because there's a lot of good poker players out there. You might say, it's really going to be a Hollywood Poker Club. But how good would it be to have a tournament online—say 100 people, and if you've won your satellite on our site, all of a sudden you're playing in a tournament, possibly, with celebrities like Jimmy Woods, Ben Affleck, Leo DiCaprio, Tobey Maguire—and many other celebrities who are good poker players. And you as a player have a chance to bust them out.

There will be many special prizes for people that bust out a celebrity. There will be also many other promotions surrounding celebrities, including such things as cruises, land based tournaments, charity events, and parties.

But the bottom line is that you can sit and play poker for a while with a guy or a girl you admire in the movie business and it's kinda fun. But believe me, when I play on that site I'm really playing as hard as I can, and I don't want people going around saying, 'I busted Jimmy Woods'. I'm gonna be nice to my fans, but I'm gonna take them for everything they've got.

Playing Poker with Celebrities

Do you have a Hollywood archrival in Poker?

I have to say Ben Affleck, and I play Ben a lot. Ben's a really good player. Annie Duke's really helped him a lot. He knows all the math—but I can still tell when Ben is bluffing and when he's not. He's an excellent, excellent player, but I can read him. We go back and forth but when it comes to the big hand and he goes in big, I can tell whether I should lay down or not. The reason I can read him so well is that I like him so much—he's a genuinely likeable guy. There's a kindness to him that I really like and I get to know it at the poker table. His father, Tim, was the reason I became an actor. His father was the stage manager at the theatre company in Boston when I was at MIT. When Ben was growing up his dad used to say, 'You know, I was the reason Jimmy Woods became an actor,' and Ben used to be like: 'Yeah sure' and think: 'Why would my dad say that? It's so embarrassing; why does he dream like that? It's so silly.' But one day Ben and Matt Damon happened to be up at my agency . . . they were with my agent, Toni

Howard, and I happened to call the office when they were there and Toni said Ben Affleck was in her office. And since Affleck isn't a common name I asked her to ask him if he knew a Tim Affleck, and he said, 'Yeh, he's my dad.' I said, 'Put him on the phone.' He said, 'Hello Mr Woods, it's an honour to meet you,' and I said, 'Did your dad ever tell you he's the reason I became an actor?'

It was like a moment in a movie. His father, who he always gently kidded, suddenly became a giant in his eyes. It was a really important moment and Ben and I have been great friends since the second we met.

What's a typical Ben Affleck Tell?

I don't wanna say 'cause I don't want him to lose any money. I'm just going to say he has a glaring tell, and I haven't told him about it yet; and it involves his head and how he holds it,—maybe . . . ha ha ha.

Acting and Poker

Does being an actor help you play the game? Does it help you control your emotions?

I was playing in a ring game with Chris Moneymaker, Amir Vahedi and some other guys who were really good. Chris had A K and I had K 4 off suit and I was on the big blind and a King and an Ace camera on the flop. Chris bet three hundred, and I came over, with a thousand, and he was like: 'Oh f—' and he laid down his hand and said, 'I had the King,' and I said: 'Oh, I had one too,' and he said: 'God you outplayed me dammit.'

So now I get pocket fives, and the flop is ace, jack, five— so I bet big—and everyone else is—fold, fold, fold, fold, fold— and I hear a call from Amir Vahedi. So in my mind I'm thinking he's got the top two pair. I'm thinking: this is perfect he's got the ace and Jack. As long as I don't see an Ace or a Jack on the turn or the river, I'm home free. So boom! On the turn, I bet, Amir calls. We get to the river, I go all in and he turns over pocket Aces, and I said: 'You mother f—er, you are so smooth,' and we became friends that night. But he was so smooth I never saw those Aces coming.

What's the best poker scene in a movie?

I think the final scene in *The Cincinnati Kid*; I like that. I think the problem with *Rounders* is that they've got to make the tell with the Oreo cookie so obvious—so the audience gets what a tell is. It was cool, but not realistic.

Confessions of an Underground Poker Junkie

Alice H. Kim

A poker player in Manhattan finds that underground card clubs are not the seedy, smoky, secretive backrooms she imagined. Informed by the movie Rounders *and by Dostoevsky's narrative* The Gambler, *the writer expected to find clubs filled with tough guys and "Russian mobsters." While she was correct that most of the patrons are men, she finds some Manhattan poker clubs that are well-lit, non-smoking, and frequented mostly by college students and young professionals. An entrepreneur tells the writer of his plans to open an upscale club in downtown Manhattan, close to Wall Street, and his hopes that his place might attract the type of clientele that once played at the famous Mayfair club.*

I walk down a dark, damp alley keeping my eyes peeled for number 225. A cement staircase leads me down to a subterranean-level door. I look up at the camera and wave while the heavy, paint-chipped door buzzes open. As I reach for the doorknob, I instinctively look behind my shoulder to make sure no one is watching me. The door closes behind me. There is no turning back. I've just entered an underground card room in New York City.

But there's just one thing. The above scenario is the result of a wildly overactive imagination. My imagination.

Card Club Reality

When I first heard about underground card clubs in Manhattan, I immediately conjured up images of smoky, somber back room dens, filled with Russian mobsters and Eastern European cocktail waitresses; part *Rounders*, part Dostoevsky's *The*

Alice H. Kim, "The Poker Scene in NYC: Confessions of an Underground Poker Junkie," *Bluff*, June-July 2005. Reproduced by permission.

Gambler. So it was quite a surprise when my friend Joe took me to my first underground outing. No eerie, shadowy alleyways. No stairwells leading to basement level rooms. No secret passwords. And, because this is New York City, there was no smoking happening—anywhere. Why should an illegal poker club pay any heed to the city's anti-smoking policy? Because, according to the owner of this particular club located on the Upper East Side, "We're not strictly legal, but we're not necessarily illegal either." While the exact laws of gambling in New York are unclear, it's undoubtedly one of the city's fastest growing enterprises—around a half-dozen places have opened within the past year alone.

Steve Addison has been running his Upper East Side club located, ironically, in an elevator building—not in some dungeon-level room—since the late 1990s. "I like to think of my club as a place for social game-playing. It's not just about poker and playing for money, it's where people come to socialize and have fun playing cards with new faces."

On any given night you can expect to find between 50–100 players competing in the club's daily tournaments. With the boom of televised poker, such as the World Poker Tour, Poker Superstars and coverage of the World Series of Poker on ESPN, Steve has seen a vast increase in players, especially within the past year. "I've seen about a 20% a month increase in players since October 2003." Even Chris Moneymaker has sat down at one of the nine green felt tables available in this brightly lit establishment.

The Usual Suspects

On this particular rainy Sunday afternoon, there are around 40 players, ranging in age from 20–35. The ratio of men to women is about 16:1. We're talking a lot of testosterone. Not bad for a single, Manhattan girl like me. But I'm not here to find myself a date (Okay, maybe sometimes), I'm here to play some cards and hope that, unlike my first venture a year ago, I don't lose my whole tournament stack holding onto a lousy pair.

Since it's the weekend, the crowd is mostly from the neighborhood (twenty-somethings from the Upper East Side) and fairly collegiate, though some may argue it's more like Collegiate, the tiny private high school on Manhattan's Upper West Side.

"We i.d. at the door. You've got to be 18 in order to gamble in the state of New York," says Addison. That's certainly not the way these clubs want to get shut down—for promoting underage gambling—so most of them adhere to a strict age enforcement door policy.

So I find myself surrounded by guys in Diesel jeans, Yankees baseball caps and Abercrombie long-sleeved T-shirts. I chuckle as I hear someone say, "You're like the Unabomber!" to one guy sitting at my table in a gray hooded sweatshirt and sunglasses. Knowing Phil Laak personally, all I want to say is, "I know 'the Unabomber' and you're no Unabomber." But I restrain myself. I look around the room and notice that, apart from the female dealer, I'm the only girl in the room. With more women getting interested in the game, those numbers should start changing, but I have to admit, I kind of like these odds.

The percentage is even lower at another club across the Park. This card club, which opened within the past year on Manhattan's Upper West Side, is located in yet another nondescript elevator building. With around twelve tables split between two rooms, it's a larger spread than Addison's place, but the ratio of men to women is about 30:1. Talk about a men's club. Looking around, the average age looks to be around 26, which seems right on target when you notice guys like Joe Cassidy, John D'Agostino, David Williams and Antonio Esfandiari making a name for themselves in their early to mid-twenties. And since it's a weeknight, the crowd is decisively more business-like—a mixture of guys in suits fresh off work at various law firms ('No breaking the law here!'), brokerage houses and the like. Definitely not the picture of underground poker I imagined a year ago. But while today's New York City underground clubs are well lit, clean and more-or-less safe, they don't compare to the club of years past, the Mayfair.

Clubs Old and New

Rudy Giuliani shut down this legendary cardroom around the same time as the topless bars and the shows along 42nd Street that gave Times Square its rakish charm and character (before it became New York City's version of Disneyland, or worse yet, Minnesota's Mall of America). It was at the Mayfair in the 1980s that players like Howard Lederer, Erik Seidel and Steve Zolotow grinded away for hours upon hours, hoping to flop trips and make kings full on the river. This was at a time when No Limit Texas Hold'em wasn't the only game in town. Now it's just about the only game offered today. All joints run No Limit Hold'em tournaments and, as players get knocked out, the cash tables begin to form. With most of the tables running $1/$2, we're not exactly talking about high-stakes *Rounders* poker, but with increased interest and players becoming (gasp!) better players, the desire for larger games is starting to surface. And it's for this reason that Eric Beacon, a former Wall Street/backgammon/poker player, has set his sights on opening, "a place where I would want to go and play. It's about time there's a club to replace what the Mayfair used to be."

Ah, the Mayfair. The card club that was immortalized in *Rounders*. "They made the Chesterfield [the name of the club in the movie] much darker and seedier than the Mayfair actually was," says Beacon. "In reality, the Mayfair was a safe, professional and pleasant place to play cards. They had great poker games at a variety of stakes, backgammon, high-tech security, a computerized database that checked each player in, and they had great food to boot."

He's hoping that his new club, slated to open in May 2005, will attract a more mature clientele—perhaps even some of those players who used to frequent the Mayfair. "I'm looking to have a full house of around 100 players here on our first night," he says.

It looks like he won't have a hard time finding players, because, as they say in real estate: 'location, location, location'. And for Beacon, the location of his new club can't be beat: downtown Manhattan in close proximity, not only to my apartment (thank God!), but also some of the biggest players around: the finance guys on Wall Street. "I'm really excited about the possibility of having a weekday game with brokers and traders coming in right after the whistle blows [the market closes at 4:02 p.m.]. These are guys who are looking to mix up their home and office games. Plus, they'd prefer to be dealt by professional dealers instead of playing poker in a back office room, hiding from their supervisors."

While downtown poker clubs aren't exactly a novel concept, Beacon is hoping to cash in on his venture by creating a more upscale club. "There's a real need for a place that caters to the Wall Street crowd. These guys want a place that feels like a club they feel comfortable in—like a members only situation."

He has a point. There are plenty of card clubs in lower Manhattan, but not the sort of places I would feel comfortable in. Chinatown, for instance, has its fair share of secret card rooms, but I wouldn't want to frequent them alone at night. As a taxi driver who told me about one of the places on Catherine near East Broadway put it: "I wouldn't want to go there myself, and I'm a guy!"

Taking a tour of Beacon's soon-to-be poker club, located in a three-story townhouse, I am told to imagine six tables on the ground floor where most of the low-limit games will take place. The second floor will be a lounge area with a pool table, some backgammon tables, a large-screen television and kitchen for light snacks and drinks. The third floor will be host to two or three tables for private V.I.P. (read: higher-stakes) rotation games, where players can choose between Hold'em, Omaha and lesser-known games like Deuce to Seven Triple Draw. As I leave the building and shake this budding entrepreneur's hand goodbye, I can't help but think: It's time to start building my bankroll now.

CHAPTER 2

The Struggles of
Gambling Addicts

How I Was Snared by Online Gambling

Maureen Paton

Like many people struggling with an addiction, the anonymous speaker in the following piece wishes to remain just that— anonymous. She is identified only as a "divorced mother, aged 49." Her problems began when her father became seriously ill and she became his main caregiver. On a friend's recommendation, she bought a computer to keep her company during the evenings. Although she was not very good with computers, she soon discovered an appealing Web site filled with bright colors and flashing lights. It was an online casino.

After her father died, she found herself gambling online, sometimes for eight hours at a time. She would get so engrossed that she would forget to eat and spend all night sipping wine and gambling. The writer says that online gambling was her way of seeking solace from loneliness, stress, and grief. She finally broke her habit by installing a program that denies access to gambling sites.

*I*nternet gambling is booming and women now account for more than half of those placing bets online. One divorced mother, age 49, tells Maureen Paton how the occasional flutter in the comfort of her own home spiralled into a dangerous addiction.

Online gambling is like a drug. In my experience, it brings out the same sort of feelings: obsession, euphoria, despair and withdrawal symptoms. I started internet gambling two and a half years ago, during the last six months of my father's life. I had already left my job to look after him when he became seriously ill. Soon I began to suffer from insomnia with all the stress. He was my only family, apart from my 29-year-old daughter—my mother died 20 years ago and I divorced in my 20s—so we were particularly close and I was determined not to hand him over to carers. Eventually he was hospitalised, but I still spent a lot of time at his bedside and did all his laundry.

A friend . . . suggested I buy a computer to keep me company in the small hours. I wasn't great with computers, but I managed to contact some old school friends online and I was surprised at how much I enjoyed surfing the internet. One day a leaflet came through the door with a website address for online casinos and I decided to take a look. The site was incredibly easy to access all I had to do was give my debit card details and I was in with just a couple of clicks of the mouse.

The sites are designed to appeal to complete beginners—the flashy, bright look of the page makes you feel like you're playing some kind of children's game. Just being on the site gave me this sense of not being so alone. It was as if I was part of a cosy online community and the whole thing felt very reassuring. I think, as a woman, I found gambling online particularly attractive because I was in the safest of environments: the comfort of my own home.

I took to playing the online slot machines, mainly because they are a matter of luck, not skill—much easier than poker or betting on horses. It's not like being surrounded by beery men in some seedy arcade; in fact, the whole thing felt quite glamorous. At the beginning I wasn't betting that much though sometimes I would lose 50 [British] pounds at the push of a button. But paying in plastic made it seem much more unreal, because you forget you're spending money.

An Inheritance

Things got seriously out of control when Dad passed away.

He left me a six-figure sum of money, together with a pile of his share papers. Suddenly, I found myself with money to spare. It had always been a dream of mine to move to the West Country, so, although it meant leaving my daughter and most of my friends, I bought a house in Devon last year. I wanted to make a fresh start away from the noise and traffic of London. A friend moved down with me: we planned to run a bed-and-breakfast business together. But we hadn't given ourselves time to research the region properly, and we had to abandon our BB idea after realising the place was too remote to attract many customers. And it wasn't long before my friend was woken up one night by the slot-machine music coming from my bedroom. She was horrified to discover my secret and couldn't understand that I didn't seem to have any power over my addiction. She soon moved back to London and her old job.

With the increased isolation, the online addiction really kicked in: I felt I was living in a bubble. Within two months of moving to Devon, my computer had become a lethal weapon and my home a prison. I would be online for up to eight hours at a time. Online gambling can easily be 24/7 if you want it to be. I got completely locked into that virtual world: I would even forget to do ordinary, necessary things such as eating. I would just sit there all night sipping wine, glued to the screen. When you win, the machine blasts upbeat music at you, and I would get such an incredible buzz that I couldn't tear myself away and I was absolutely euphoric; the next day I would be in tears after realising how much I had lost during the night.

The money goes quickly because of the sheer speed of the games and because you are totally engrossed as if on a roller-coaster of emotion. I found that it wasn't difficult to get rid of 2,000 pounds in a few hours; it makes me feel sick even just saying that. Eventually I was losing up to 5,000 pounds in a weekend.

Bombarded by Offers

On one website, I made the mistake of getting too friendly with the managers after telephoning their support line with a question about cash limits. I began telling them my life story because they seemed so sympathetic.

Eventually I was getting bombarded with weekly promotional emails from them, offering me the chance to gamble on their other sites.

They were like vultures, hooking me in; they would offer me 30 per cent credit for every 100 pounds I gambled.

I racked up a big overdraft and only managed to clear it by selling the house for a profit just four months after I'd bought it. I downsized to a smaller house in an even more isolated area of Devon. Over the summer, I finally realised it had to stop when I started smoking again because of all the worry. I got distraught about the money I was losing. I kept seeing myself ending up in the gutter. I couldn't face coming forward and asking for help from Gamblers Anonymous because that meant publicly admitting I was an addict. But when I did finally pluck up courage and ring them, I discovered that I lived too far away from their nearest meeting place. So I looked for other helplines in the telephone directory and saw an advertisement for the advice organisation Gamcare. I contacted them and was told about a software package called Gamblock.

Drastic Step

After you've installed it, you can't access gambling sites any more, otherwise your computer will immediately refuse to function.

It was a drastic step but I needed something drastic and so far it has worked for me. It has been nearly a month since I last placed a bet.

I'm going to sell up for the second time soon and move back to London, where I can see more of my daughter and my old friends. Even though I haven't got a lot of my father's legacy left, I am beginning to feel in control of myself at last. In retrospect, I think I haven't grieved properly for my father and I haven't been thinking clearly. The past few years have been a particularly vulnerable time in my life. When sad things happen to you, you have to find your escape: gambling has been mine.

I Am a Lottery Ticket Addict

Chris Wright

For Chris Wright, the world of gambling had always been exciting and exotic. He loved all types of betting, collected gambling memorabilia, and used to be proud of being a gambler. However, in this selection he describes his humiliation at realizing that he is addicted to scratch lottery tickets. He begs for money from his father, lies to his wife, and speculates about taking up a life of crime. It is only after what he describes as "a manic episode" of buying and scratching tickets that he realizes that he has a problem. The hardest part about quitting, he writes, is facing the fact that he has lost a lot of money that he will not get back.

It's not easy to say these words. I—am—an—addict. A screw-up. A sucker. A sicko. I cannot be trusted. I need help. I cannot help myself. These were a few of the topics kicked around recently when my wife and my father came at me with a sort of mini-intervention—like a surprise party, but with self-help books instead of balloons. There were cups of tea involved, a lot of *whys* and *how could yous*. There was talk of "healing" and "support." It would have been laughable if it weren't so final.

See, I didn't want to stop. Didn't even want to think about it. But I didn't have much choice in the matter. I'm an addict, and addicts don't choose.

I used to feel a certain amount of pride in being a gambler. I imagined it gave my life a touch of glamour, a bit of danger. And I loved it. Some of the happiest nights of my life have been spent in Reno and Vegas and Deadwood, South Dakota. I have visited ratty two-table shanties and wandered the glistening halls of Foxwoods and Mohegan Sun. I have dreamed of shooting craps in Monte Carlo, a martini in hand, a mountain of multicolored chips before me. I would register massive shifts in fortune with a cocked eyebrow. Maybe I would draw a crowd.

Even penny-ante games get me going—the rounds of cribbage, gin, and liar's poker at my local bar. I have gambled on soccer matches, horse races, card cuts, coin tosses, and games of pool. I once bet on who could hold a lit match the longest. The game doesn't matter, nor the venue, nor the stake. What matters is the chase, pitting myself against the unfathomable forces of luck. It's almost a spiritual thing.

My office contains a little shrine to gambling. I have ashtrays and cocktail trays emblazoned with hearts and diamonds, clubs and spades. I have an antique roulette wheel. A mug with a picture of a guy chasing a donkey: I lost my ass in Vegas. A key ring that says crazy for craps. I have Bakelite chips, novelty playing cards, and dice, dice, dice. One Christmas, my mother-in-law bought me a book, *The Quotable Gambler*. I already owned it. Gambling isn't just a passion, it's part of who I am. It's *me*.

Discovering Scratch Tickets

Despite all this, the gambling never felt out of control. At least not until I started playing scratch tickets. That was when I set out on the road to feckless, lolloping loserdom. That was when I started jerking my friends around—standing them up because I'd lost all my money, or borrowing cash, or cadging drinks. That was when I started lying to my wife. Scratch tickets ate up the rent money and earned me a reputation as a flake. Scratch tickets had me banging my head against walls, gurgling with remorse. Scratch tickets.

Monte Carlo seems a long way off now. I'm a scratcher, and there's not much glamour in that. Ever see James Bond huddled in the corner of a 7-Eleven, working away at a Reindeer Games? [Actor] Omar Sharif nicking the surface of a

Lucky Lady Bugs? Did [novelist] Fyodor Dostoyevsky sneak out in the middle of the night to procure a bundle of Tic Tac Doe? Of course not. Scratch tickets are a mug's game. And I am the mug.

There's a hierarchy in the gaming world—a gambler's caste system. People who play poker look down on people who play blackjack who look down on people who go to the track who look down on people who play slots who look down on people who play Keno who look down on people who play scratch tickets who look down on . . . bingo players? Perhaps. As a scratch addict, I'm pretty much at the bottom of the heap. *Hey, Grandma, why don't you play a real game?*

Government in the Gambling Business

But I'm not alone. In 2000, nearly $148 million was bet on the lottery in Maine—$107 million just on scratch tickets.

As David Nibert points out in his recent book, *Hitting the Lottery Jackpot: State Governments and the Taxing of Dreams*, that scratch tickets are a particularly insidious game. They are lovely to look at, they are easily accessible, they allow rapid-fire betting, and, as Nibert writes, they offer people with limited prospects "a *new opportunity* for individual economic advancement."

The most dangerous thing about these tickets, though, is that they don't really feel like gambling. They certainly don't feel like the life-crushers they can become. In fact, you're doing a *good* thing by playing them. The Maine State Lottery doled out over $38 million in 2000 to local cities and towns. That's over $3 million a month. Buy a loaf of bread and a Tic Tac Doe ticket, and some potholes in Gray get fixed. No smoky casino to go to, no grim-faced bookie. How bad could it be?

Actually pretty bad. For one thing, since it introduced them in 1974, the state lottery has raised the ante on its scratch tickets. Fifty cent tickets were phased-out in 1982 and the state introduced $2, $3, and $5 tickets in the 1990s. Scratch tickets, regardless of their shiny, just-a-bit-of-fun veneer, are high-stakes gambling. At $5 a ticket you could be out $50 in the space of a cigarette. I, of all people, should know.

Hitting Bottom

The day before I was so lovingly shanghaied by my family, I'd hit rock bottom with my habit. At least I hope so. Any lower and I'd taste oil. It was a Friday afternoon. I was scratching, as I often do on Friday afternoons, flush with the spoils of direct deposit, eager to escape the stresses and responsibilities of the work week. I'd had bad gambling bouts before. I'd bitched my way through spells of deplorable luck. But this one was different. Something snapped.

I was playing the scratch tickets, and losing at a rat-a-tat rate. I wasn't having fun. This wasn't a "bit of a flutter." Word was that this particular game offered the best odds ever of getting a big hit. My reasoning—if you can call it that—was that before I quit these damn things for good, I'd have one last shot at getting back the thousands of dollars I'd squandered in the past. I wanted closure. And once I started, I couldn't stop. I was having what the experts call a "manic episode." I couldn't stop.

I'd say the $200 mark was the point where common sense and desire finally parted company. I took out another hundred, then another. I couldn't have been any less in control if I'd swallowed a fistful of acid and washed it down with a bottle of tequila. My head had been shot from a cannon. My will was a wet rag snagged on the bumper of a bus. I was heading straight for Brokesville and there wasn't a thing I could do about it.

Looking back on that episode now is like trying to watch a tennis match through a keyhole. The picture's blurry and incomplete. I know that I was hot-faced, fizzing. I know I fumbled the last crinkly 10-spot from my pocket and handed it over to the guy behind the counter. I know the guy was bald. My last 10 bucks. But imagine—*imagine!*—if I had scored. I could have had a happy ending. I handed the money over. I remember that.

Breaking Down

It was an ending all right, but not a happy one. Broke, I called my dad and asked for a loan. I said something about needing to pay off some debts. I promised I'd pay him back. I all but begged him to lend me the money. I all but wept. When he said no, I slammed down the phone. I called him back. I slammed down the phone. I called him back. I told him I needed help. I said it: I am an addict.

Aren't I?

I am now the owner of a Gamblers Anonymous handbook, a little yellow pamphlet with that "God grant me the serenity" poem printed on the cover. "How can you tell whether you are a compulsive gambler?" the handbook asks. It goes on to list 20 questions: "Have you ever felt remorse after gambling?"—yes—"Did you ever gamble longer than you had planned?"—yes—"Did you often gamble until your last dollar was gone?"—hell, yes. If you answer in the affirmative to seven of the twenty questions, you are probably a compulsive gambler. My score is 15.

Okay, so how did I get to this point?

The Route to Addiction

Since that spectacularly grim day, I've done some research. Turns out, the path I took to addiction is a well-worn one. If you were to chart the route to compulsive gambling, it might go something like this:

- **The Joy Luck Club.** You tee-hee your way through a few bucks here and there. Win a little, lose a little—no big deal.

- **The Bait.** About 50 percent of problem gamblers report getting a big win early on in their gambling careers. Tee-hees turn to knee-trembling oh-jeezes.

- **The Bite**. Eager to relive the rush of that early win, Gambler starts laying bigger bets with more frequency. Losses are brushed aside in anticipation of the next delicious hit.

- **Momentum**. As losses begin to accumulate, Gambler stops playing to recapture past glory and starts playing catch-up. Anticipation gives way to a creeping sense of desperation.

- **Free Fall**. Ever-larger bets are placed in an effort to recoup losses. When the all-important wins fail to materialize, Gambler responds with self-loathing, anger, and manic determination.

- **The Monster**. The habit grows to unmanageable proportions. Gambler starts borrowing from friends and family, devising elaborate lies to cover up losses. Gambler rationalizes. Can stop any time.

- **The Felon**. Unable to wring any more money from friends, family, and colleagues, Gambler engages in fraud, theft, and other illegal acts. Borrows from loan sharks.

- **The Bust**. Gambler's relationships start to break down. Loved ones lay down ultimatums, or just pack up and leave. Lonely and racked with guilt, Gambler gets sick, depressed.

- **Endgame**. Gambler gets caught cheating or stealing. Facing prison, divorce, and perhaps broken legs, Gambler hits rock bottom, considers ending it all. Twenty percent of card-carrying problem gamblers say they have attempted suicide.

I cringe when I think how closely this model applies to my story—right down to the early hit ($1,000 on a $2 ticket). The discovery that I'm not alone should be comforting. It isn't.

The fact that my sky-lowering drama is so run-of-the-mill, so *predictable*, is somehow even more demeaning.

At the same time, I'm grateful that I stopped when I did (edging into the "Monster" stage). There are gamblers out there who make my habit look like a penchant for coin collecting: the guy who stole money from his daughter's piggy bank; the guy who went to the racetrack on the day his wife died of cancer; the guy who stole $300,000 from his law firm, got caught, and killed himself on the eve of his son's 11th birthday. There is some comfort in the thought that I wasn't *that* bad.

On the other hand, I was pretty bad.

Criminal Intents

The scariest moment of my brush with ruin came when I began to entertain thoughts of committing a crime. I wasn't about to rob a bank, mug an old lady, or start giving hand jobs at my local bus terminal, but I had eyed a thick stack of scratch tickets at a convenience store, and I had thought how nice it would be if I could only . . . It was the *if* that saved me. That and a big fat yellow streak.

When people associate addiction with crime, they tend to think of sweat-slick crackheads lifting Pampers from Stop & Shops, cankerous junkies pulling blades in gloomy alleyways, or bloated alcos kicking the crap out of each other in parking lots. But hard-line gamblers are as likely to resort to crime as any drug addict. In fact, given the limitless amounts of money that can be poured into their addiction, they may be even more so.

Forty-seven percent of people in Gamblers Anonymous (GA), for instance, say that they have engaged in fraud or theft. Thirty-two percent of prison inmates acknowledge having a gambling problem. David Nibert, citing a nationwide study on state-sponsored gambling, writes that "states with lotteries had a rate of property crimes about 3 percent higher than states without, a statistically significant finding." Yet it's unlikely that someone who discovers his car missing or her house burgled will spit out, "Damn *scratch* addicts!"

The Gambler and the Rush

Part of this misconception stems from the fact that many people have trouble thinking of gambling as an addiction at all. It's something you *do*, not something you take. A recent study at Harvard Medical School, however, found that a gambler's brain responds to a bet in much the same way a drug user's responds to a line of coke. The hormones released during a gambling bout produce a real chemical high. But you don't have to be a neurologist to know this. All you need is to have slapped down a 10-spot on an all-or-nothing scratch ticket.

But where's the buzz in that? How could I possibly get a kick out of frittering my money away? Questions like these point to another error non-gamblers make when trying to understand people like me. The true gambler gets a rush just from laying down a bet, or even *thinking* of laying down a bet. And perversely, or maybe inevitably, losing makes winning all the more enjoyable.

Even Losing Is A Thrill

The tail end of a losing streak is a place of great possibility. For all the sobbing and whining, the loser knows this—at least on a subconscious level. You know that by unloading a boatload of cash you are setting yourself up for the most delirious rush a gambler can experience. And you know that the longer a losing streak lasts, the bigger the rush will be when the streak breaks.

There's an old saying among gamblers: "The biggest bet I ever made was my last two dollars." The eye-popping, heart-stopping action doesn't come when the shipping magnate slaps down a hundred thou on the spin of a roulette wheel; it comes when some poor slob hands over the dregs of a stake on a lousy ace-high. To come from behind, to pull yourself back from the brink of ruin—*that* is pure rocket fuel.

Herein lies the gambler's Catch-22: if you quit in the midst of a losing streak, you're denying yourself the Big Bang that comes when you finally break out of it. And if you're on a winning streak—well, what kind of idiot stops in the middle of a winning streak? Couple this dilemma with the physical addiction of gambling, and it's clear why, according to some estimates, as many as 92 percent of addicts suffer at least one relapse.

But not me. I'm stopping.

Lies Gamblers Tell Themselves

A seasoned gambler, if you say something like this, will laugh in your face. Compulsive gamblers are liars. And long before they start lying to their spouses and co-workers and friends, they lie to themselves. They say things like "Not me" and "I'm stopping." Dana Forman, associate program director at the Council on Compulsive Gambling, has a list that he sends out: "40 Lies Problem Gamblers Tell Themselves."

- *When I bet $50 and win $100, I'm up $100.*

- *It takes money to make money.*

- *I'll stop once I get even.*

- *I'm not that bad yet.*

- *Without gambling, life would be boring.*

"Without gambling, life would be boring." It's got a ring of truth to it. How *do* you replace something as all-consuming as a gambling habit? Could anything else even begin to approach the sheer drama of it all? Needlepoint and stamp collecting aren't going to cut it. Neither are movies, pinball, or long walks in the park.

Another thing people often fail to take into account is this: gamblers *love* to gamble.

Why Do People Get Addicted?

Dana Forman doesn't buy this line of reasoning at all. "An addiction isn't 'love,'" he says. "You're a slave to it. You've lost control of your own behavior. And that's not love." Forman does agree, however, that the recovering gambler faces a huge challenge in finding something to take the place of the habit. "That's one of the more common questions," he says. "'What do I do with this void in my life?' There are no easy answers. You have to figure it out for yourself."

Not surprisingly, a large number of recovering gamblers turn to religion. The second step in the GA 12-step recovery program, for instance, states, "[We] came to believe that a Power greater than ourselves could restore us to a normal way of thinking and living." In many ways, though, it was a "power greater than ourselves" that got us into this damn mess in the first place.

A friend of mine once remarked that my gambling habit stemmed from a fascination with "the point where statistics and psychology meet." But it's more than this. Gambling embodies a belief system. We *believe* in Luck. We can feel it within us: the mana that allows us to f— *know* what that next card will be. And we feel its absence. As we double-down on 11 and see a three. As we get up from the table and perform our little *oops-oops* two-steps with passersby.

Luck, as all gamblers know, is a vengeful god. So we court it. We coddle it. We adopt little rituals to appease it. Your average compulsive gambler observes a level of superstition that would put the most devout fundamentalist to shame. We have our lucky socks, our lucky shirts, our lucky numbers, our lucky dealers, our lucky drinks, our lucky seats, our lucky games, our lucky days. The very idea that "my luck has to kick in sooner or later" is magical thinking at its most basic level.

The Gambler's Belief System

The gambler's belief system is intense and immediate. When we pray, we expect our prayers to be answered, and we expect them to be answered now. And when they are, oh, we feel blessed, in the truest, most mystical sense of the word. What code have we cracked? What power have we tapped into? Nothing can compete with the thrill of having Luck on your side—not talent, not smarts, and not knuckle-down toil. It's the only true brush with faith that many of us get. But faith is, by its very nature, a fragile thing.

The day of my terrible scratch session, at the very moment I began to fathom what a mess I was in, I heard that a worker on a nearby construction site had scored $4 million on a scratch ticket. Word was he had bought the ticket from the same store I had been trawling all day. That was it. I didn't scream, I didn't spit, and I didn't shake my fist at the sky. But I no longer had any faith in Luck—at least not *my* luck. What else would I lose?

I didn't really mind telling my dad I was a gambling addict. Telling my wife, though, was another matter. I felt guilty. I felt pathetic and maggoty. More than this, I felt scared. "Oh, you know everything I've said to you over the last year? Disregard it." How the hell would she react to that?

Apparently, my fears were well-founded.

Confession Time

"It's the Watergate of gambling," says Dana Forman. "President Nixon was forced to resign not because he committed crimes, but because he tried to cover them up. It's the great cover-up that gets you into trouble."

Equally unsettling was the realization that once I made my confession, once the truth was out—well, that would be it. My love affair with gambling would have to come to an end. This too, says Forman, is a common reaction. "Many gamblers report that when the spouse threatens to leave them, they will say, 'Good, now I'll be able to gamble all I want without your nagging,'" he says. "That's what the addiction does."

But I'm lucky; owning up to addiction has actually helped my marriage. For one thing, I can finally look my wife in the eye, free of the ball-withering guilt that went with the lies and obfuscation. My "outing" has answered a lot of questions. It's given us something to focus on, something to take aim at—a common enemy. My marriage feels stronger now than it did a month ago, and next month it'll feel stronger.

I realize it now: I'm lucky.

I also realize that I not only have to stop lying, I have to stop blaming. I have to stop shifting responsibility. I have to realize that what I have long called "bad luck" was actually bad judgment. The crap I've had to deal with is not the lottery's fault. It's not the fault of the guy who bought *my* winning scratch ticket. It's not the fault of the friend who introduced me to gambling 20 years ago. It's not in my genes or my culture or my stars. *I'm* the one who gambled my money away. It's me.

Fighting Temptations

I don't even blame my former scratch-mate—we'll call him Mike—who still tries to tempt me every now and again: "Twenty'll get you in." The other day, Mike approached me with a pocket full of scratch tickets. There could be a winner, he said, a $4 million winner. I looked at the tickets fanned out in his hand—so silvery, so full of possibility. A few weeks ago, I would have succumbed to the *what if* in a heartbeat. This time, I wished him luck and walked away.

But I'm not naive enough to believe I've got this thing licked. Not yet. An addict is an addict is an addict, right? "Admission that one has a problem is the first step," says Forman. "It's a huge one, but it's not enough. You've got to keep going. There's a lot of legwork." He's right, of course: there's a lot of work left yet.

I am planning one last ritual.

I will go into my back yard, take a dollar bill from my pocket, and set it on fire. As I watch the bill burn, I'll say a few words for all the money I've spent on gambling in the last few years. Ashes to ashes, scratch to scratch. This private ceremony, I hope, will help me break the spell once and for all.

For me, the hardest part of quitting has been coming to terms with a single, simple fact: the money I've lost is money I've lost. It's not money I've yet to win back. It's not money I've invested. I haven't been putting good luck aside on the layaway plan. There will be no redress, no redeeming hit. "You have to let go," says Forman. "You're never going to get that money back, ever." This is the most excruciating thing to do, to let go of hope like that. It's the hardest part.

About a month after I stopped gambling, my wife and I went to see a movie. I didn't try to wriggle out of paying for the tickets. I bought the candy *and* the soda. I remember thinking, "That's a bloody stupid thing to be proud of." Anyway, it was a far cry from the Thames-side penthouse I'd hoped to own, or the round-the-world trip I'd hoped to go on. Then, as the lights dimmed and the movie started, my wife gave my hand a little squeeze. I will never win the jackpot. I will never go to Monte Carlo. There are other things to hope for.

I Am in Residential Treatment for My Gambling

David

The author of the following piece is a young man known only as David. David describes how he began gambling on a British slot machine called a "fruit machine" when he was a young boy. As a teenager he spent most of his time at the local snooker hall (a British pool parlor) and playing the fruit machines with big payouts. At college, he was more interested in the local dog track than in his studies, and he dropped out halfway through his second year. When he took a job as a cashier to a bookie, his problems worsened. He was deeply in debt and working twelve-hour shifts to try to pay off what he owed.

David eventually entered the Gordon House Association, a treatment and support center for addicted gamblers in England. At the time this article was written, David had lived at the center for six months and was hopeful that his recovery would last.

They say that you never see a poor bookmaker, well; I have the dubious honour of being the exception! I spent five years on the 'right' side of the betting shop counter taking the punter's [a bettor] money. The trouble was I couldn't wait to gamble my own money and any other cash I could get my hands on. I left the industry two years ago, due to the stress of working 12 hour shifts knowing that my wages were merely paying off gambling debts.

Gambling had always fascinated me. I used to love playing the fruit machines [British slot machines] as a kid when my dad gave me a few pound coins to play with (my only ever 'no lose' gamble).

I didn't know what I was doing, but who cared? It was a buzz. By the time that I was 16 years of age I was introduced

David, "The Next Jimmy White?," *GamCare Matters*, Summer 2004, p. 9. Reproduced by permission.

to the murky world of the local snooker [a variation of pool] hall. It was the £200 [about $335] Jackpot fruit machines there that grabbed my attention. Within a fortnight of playing the machines I hit the jackpot. I won £168 [about $300]. I felt ecstatic, I was hooked.

Skipping School

My 'A' level studies took a back seat as I missed lessons to go to the snooker hall—all my cash going into the machines. I remember nearly running a woman down after I went through a red light. I was speeding back from the cash point in my haste to put more money in the fruit machine, to chase my losses. I spent that much time in the snooker hall that my mum thought that I was going to be the new Jimmy White [a popular British snooker player]!

I managed to jumble my way through my 'A' levels and ended up at university. Rather than follow the usual student rituals, I was making my way to the local dog track three nights a week. Inside of two months I had lost my student grant, loan and savings. I was betting £20 [about $35] a race when students were meant to live on £40 [about $71] a week. But, I was flash and loved to bet big—win or lose. The book-makers at the track must have loved me; they would have shed a collective tear the day I left university.

I dropped out of university halfway through my second year. I'd been to one lecture in five months. I'd learnt nothing about the economist John Maynard Keynes, but I had plenty of ideas about the 3.07 race at Milton Keynes! So, I moved back home and carried on in the same vein for six months.

A Job in Gambling

I virtually lived in my local bookies, so it was a logical pro-gression when I took a job as a cashier there. Suddenly, I was being paid to be in the place I'd been in all day anyway. I couldn't believe my luck. For a few months I stayed gambling free, simply happy to watch the races from behind the counter. Then I started getting my friends to put bets on for me and eventually I'd just write them out myself. I'd lose my month's wages in the shop the day I got paid.

Every month I promised myself that the next month would be different but it never was. Even after gaining a promotion to shop manager I was still the same. That was the pattern for three years before I left to go travelling to Australasia [the area that includes Australia, New Zealand and New Guinea] for a year. I knew that I would be going to Australasia so somehow I managed to put money aside for my trip. I received some help from my family as well. Even over there I managed to gamble the £2,000 [about $3,500] I had for my trip in four days in a casino. It meant that I was picking fruit for a year to scrape by, even sleeping rough and ending up in court for non-payment of rent.

On my return from travelling I went to work for another bookmaker in the City of London. I had hoped that I had learnt my lesson, but I was wrong. Within six months I had lost £10,000 [about $17,000] all owed on credit cards and loans. After a year I simply resigned my post as I was fed up working 12 hours shifts just to pay my debts. The day before I quit I lost £1,000 [about $1,700] in an afternoon. For the next year I was back on the wrong side of the counter gambling whatever cash I could get my hands on.

The Bailiffs At My Door

Obviously, I had ignored all of my debts and had the bailiffs at my door all of the time. I couldn't pay them. I could see no solution, so I took an overdose to end it all. My mum found me and I was rushed to hospital. I spent a fortnight in a psychiatric unit recovering. I was referred to GA [Gamblers Anonymous] but I telephoned GamCare instead. I was put in touch with Gordon House, a residential treatment centre for compulsive gamblers.

I have been living there now for six months out of a nine month duration. Apart from a few weeks in October, I have remained gambling free and I feel great. I cannot wait to face the future, knowing that if I can conquer this, my life will be better and the lives of those around me who I have hurt will be better too.

I feel liberated, but I know I will be fighting this for the rest of my life. But, it is a battle that I know I am going to win.

My Brother Was a Compulsive Gambler

Michelle Wong

After Michelle Wong's brother Phillip committed suicide, Wong coped with her grief in the best way she knew how—she made a film. She traveled to Las Vegas, interviewed her brother's family and friends, and uncovered a story of a gambling addiction that had spiraled out of control. Before his death at age thirty-six, Phillip was binge gambling and stealing from his mother and had served a stint in prison. Wong's documentary film on Phillip, Pieces of a Dream: A Story of Gambling, *premiered at the Calgary International Film Festival in September 2003. The following is an edited transcript of her voice-over narration and comments from the film, which describe Phillip's descent into gambling addiction. Wong spent a long time denying that Phillip was a compulsive gambler, but his suicide made her realize how serious his problem had been.*

Wong is also the producer and director of Return Home, *a documentary about returning to her hometown to become reacquainted with her aging grandparents. She is the executive director at the New University Television Society, a community access television production facility in Calgary, and is currently producing two independent films.*

My brother was 36 years old when he committed suicide. The first reaction from the family was not to talk about his death. That somehow in that silence, the shame of what happened would fade away.

He was a father with two young children. After he died, the police came around asking me questions. Phillip hadn't left a suicide note and I began to wonder if he really had

Michelle Wong, "Pieces of a Dream: A Story of Gambling," *Alberta Views*, November-December 2004, pp. 44–45. Reproduced by permission of the author.

killed himself. My family wanted to bury the tragedy and move on, but I couldn't stop thinking about him.

When you grow up in a fragmented family, you learn to accept the secrets. I wanted to start asking questions. I had to talk to everyone: my family, my brother's ex-wife, my stepfather, Phillip's best friend. I hoped that by gathering these pieces together, I could begin to understand what happened to him.

A Normal Childhood

St. Paul, Alberta, wasn't just where my brother died; it's where our story began.

My family owned a Chinese restaurant on main street. It was our second home. My sister worked the cash register and waited on tables. My brother and I helped out in the kitchen with my mom. A break to the routine would come every Sunday when my father would take us to Edmonton to eat dim sum. My brother and I would have contests to see who could eat the most sticky rice wraps. He still holds the record at seven. I guess I would say we had a normal childhood.

Things changed for me significantly in 1980. My mother and father split up; it was a turning point in my life. Suddenly everything that had made sense didn't make sense. I think the way I took it and the way my brother took it were very different. We lived in the same house and we saw each other every day, but we never actually sat down and talked to each other about what we were feeling and what it was like to have my mother leave.

My mother eventually remarried and settled in Las Vegas. In the middle of his second year of university, my brother quit school and joined my mother. He never told me why he left and I never asked.

When Phillip arrived in Vegas, he worked odd jobs and helped my mother run her gift store. They also had a cheque cashing business, so he used to be a runner. I think the things my brother learned in Vegas were "street smart" things. But he didn't go to school; he didn't develop any particular kind of career. He was a Jack of all trades. My brother had a lot of charm. People liked him.

Apparent Success

In 1994 I went to see my mom. I felt like there had been this long division between mother and daughter and I wanted to deal with my emotions and anger about her leaving. I went to Las Vegas and I stayed for about four months; I got to know my brother a bit more. He had gotten married to a Taiwanese woman named Min, who was a U.S. citizen. They had opened their own business, a beauty salon, and my brother was helping her manage it, because he was quite a smart business guy even though he hadn't gone to school. And right around that time I saw my brother . . . the amount of money he was handling at the time. Like, he would literally pull out of his pants pocket, you know, hundred dollar bills and count them off.

And I was just . . . I was really impressed. . . . At that time, Las Vegas was growing; it was a money town and hundred dollar bills were very common. . . . Money was flowing into that city like crazy. And he was part of that prosperity: wife, two kids—twins, a boy and a girl—and they had this new house. He was driving a Lexus and wearing fancy jewellery, and I think that to him he was hitting his stride in his early 30s as somebody who had everything. It was obvious that parts of his life, in terms of the American dream, were falling into place.

The First Hint of a Problem

The El Cortez is an interesting casino for me because when I would come visit, late at night Phillip would say, "Hey, let's go out and shoot some craps." The first place he would take me to is El Cortez, number one because he worked there. But number two, they have quarter craps. So we could put $10 on the table, get 40 chips and actually play a decent game. The only time I really saw my brother gamble was when he was working at El Cortez; it was his shift off and I just happened to have some money. I had $500 with me. When we went to the table I thought, "Wouldn't it be neat to see $500 worth of chips?" So I gave my brother the $500, he turned it into chips and then he started gambling right away. Within 10 minutes, it was all gone. And I was sort of in shock, you know, like, "Phillip! That was 500 of my dollars." And he just sort of— you know, he was very laissez faire about it. He said, "Oh don't worry about it. I'll pay you back."

I went back to Canada without realizing the significance that world had begun to play in his life. And I didn't realize that what I was seeing was private and that he was sharing a secret with me. I wondered who else knew?

Gambling was always part of our life growing up. It was a form of entertainment, a fun distraction. I was becoming aware that this was more than just a pastime for Phillip. When did gambling become something he couldn't control? How did it go from entertainment to something so serious? What does it take to change someone? Do they just gamble until they're destroyed? Until there's nothing? Maybe that's it. Maybe they won't stop until there's nothing. Until everything has been pawned, sold. It's like drugs. It doesn't stop until you stop.

Threats, Lies, and Guns

My brother was covering his gambling losses by telling each person a different story. He had created a huge web of deceit.

He would come see my mom and ask her for money. And he threatened her once. He wanted $5,000. My mother said no. My brother said that he would take a gun and he would shoot himself, Min and the kids if she didn't give him the money.

The gambling became really, really obvious. My brother was under a lot of pressure, I think. My mother was hiding money in a box of soap and my brother had gone over to my mother's house to do some laundry. He took the box of soap down and discovered the money. And there was about $7,000. So he took the money and he went on a huge gambling binge. People couldn't find him for three days and nights.

After that binge, my brother went back to his house. He had lost all his money. Min was having an argument with her ex-husband, Mike. She wanted him out of the house and he wouldn't go. So Min went to my brother and said, "Mike won't get out of the house." My brother went to his closet, pulled out a gun, went downstairs and shot Mike.

Mike recovered. My brother was tried and sent to prison. In prison his gambling stopped. By then, we were all afraid of Phillip. Looking back, we knew so little about what was going on in him. I thought the shooting was a jealous act, the anger toward an ex-husband, not the anger from the binge of a gambling loss.

Trying to Make Sense of It

After a year in prison, Phillip was given a choice: more jail time or deportation to Canada. He returned to St. Paul, the place he'd escaped from 20 years earlier.

Back in Alberta, Phillip reunited with our father, whom he hadn't seen in more than 15 years. Within a few months, however, he started gambling again. In a chance conversation with some of his acquaintances, I later learned he'd started selling drugs to feed his gambling habit. He fell down a slippery slope and did not return.

I think Phillip's fall from grace was a big thing for him. Maybe much more than I realized. I think, from a cultural standpoint, for Chinese people, face is very important. And I think he literally lost his face. So he ended up at the bottom.

I read in a book that over 50 per cent of people who struggle with a serious gambling addiction contemplate suicide as a way out. When I read that, I began to understand the choice my brother made. Maybe he didn't tell me about his gambling problem because he was my big brother, a person I'd looked up to all my life, and part of him didn't want me to see that he wasn't perfect. In his death, we all struggled and blamed ourselves.

It's taken me a long time to accept that my brother was a compulsive gambler, because in some ways I didn't want to see it, and in other ways I didn't want to accept what I was seeing. I have to accept it now because it's the reason he died. It's not because my parents got divorced. It's not because he wasn't working a good job. It's because he was dealing with this illness and he was dealing with it by himself.

CHAPTER 3

Working at the Casino

A Day in the Life
Behind the Tables

Jason DuVall

In the following selection Jason DuVall describes a day's work at a casino. He deals at blackjack tables, works the roulette wheel, and presides over a side-action game called Let It Ride. His customers include friendly tourists, a group of obnoxious college students, and a drunk blackjack player who gets angrier as he continues to lose. During breaks in the action, DuVall plays cards with his coworkers in the break room, thinks about lunch, and ogles a waitress. DuVall calls his article "semi-fictional" because the day he describes is a composite of real events rather than a literal record of a particular day.

Since leaving his job at the casino in 1998, DuVall has tried several other jobs, including tech support and data entry.

I get to work at 9:30 in the morning, a half-hour before my shift starts. About half of the other dealers are already in the Break Room. Several of them are playing a game called Tonk, a Gin Rummy variant. It's popular because it's fast, and you can play a half-dozen hands in a 15-minute break. I pick up my tokes (My share of the tips from the previous day) without bothering to check how much it is, and sit in for the next hand of Tonk. My luck is running good—I manage to win six dollars before it's time to go in. One of the dealers rushes in, frantic to get his tokes before we go in to relieve the Graveyard Shift. I don't understand why . . . it's not as though he can do anything with them while we're standing our shift.

We have a full crew today—nobody called in sick. This is a mixed blessing. More people means shorter stands at the tables, but also less tips. The difference on the tips is minimal, though, so I'm glad that we have the extra relief. A full crew means one-hour stands, with 15-minute breaks in between. When people call in sick, the time on the tables increases— I've had days where I was on for 2 hours between breaks.

At some unseen signal, everyone stands and makes a last-minute check of their appearance. Vest straight, hair neat, check. I'm good to go. We march downstairs to the Pit in a loose mob, chatting softly among ourselves. When we get to the end of the Pit, the talking stops, as we wait for our table assignments. The Pit Boss assigns me to open up a Blackjack table. I go stand patiently at the table, where a metal and glass rack contains the table's checks (chips).

After a few minutes, the Pit Boss comes over and unlocks the rack. We both count the checks, to make sure that there's the same amount as when the table was closed. The pit boss spreads two decks of cards on the table in front of me, and I count them to ensure that there aren't any missing cards. There never are, but we do it anyway. They're new decks, so the cards are still in order. I shuffle them a half-dozen times, then spread them out on the table again. Then I clear my hands (wave them over the table to show the cameras that I haven't palmed anything), and put them behind my back, and wait.

Morning in the Casino

The casino is slow today. I watch the few gamblers who are up this early (Yes, 10 A.M. *is* early in a casino) and the cocktail waitresses, and think deep thoughts. Like wondering what's for lunch, and what that waitress's bust size is, and whether I could get a date with her. The time passes slowly. Eventually, I feel a tap on my shoulder. I clap out and clear my hands, then step to the right, while still covering the table, until the dealer who just tapped me out steps into the spot I was just standing in. Once I'm sure that the table has been covered, I turn and walk out of the pit. I'm not being overly cautious there . . . if I walk away without making sure that my relief is in charge of the table, it's my butt on the line, not his. It's only been a half-hour, short stands early in the day are common, as they stagger the relief to ensure a steady number of dealers in the pit.

I walk back to the Break Room. We're not allowed to be anywhere else in the casino during our breaks, except the lunch room. This is supposed to prevent any collusion between players and dealers, but it also protects us from angry players, as well. There aren't enough people there right now to play Tonk. Although there actually *are* enough people, only about a third of the dealers like playing. Some don't understand it well enough, some don't like it, some just want to save their money. I get a book from my jacket, and sit down to read.

The break is over soon enough, and I go back down to the pit. I'm assigned to Roulette. Easy when there are no players . . . just keep the wheel spinning. I'm not as sharp on Roulette as I ought to be, so I run over payout tables in my head. After a while, a player comes up, sits down, and throws a $20 bill on the table. He's a regular, Old Slim, so I know without having to ask that he wants to play at the table minimum, 25 cent checks. Roulette has special checks, which are valueless away from the table. This lets us assign any value necessary for a player to play, and also lets us differentiate whose checks are whose when there are multiple players. I pull out four stacks of Blue (Old Slim's favorite color, and not usually the first color to get issued), and call out, "Change twenty." The Pit Boss calls out confirmation, and I push the checks across the table to Old Slim. While he starts laying checks all over the layout, I drop the Twenty in the box, where all real money goes.

I use my right hand to slow down the wheel (I had it spinning far too fast—that lets me go longer without having to spin it again), then pull the lighter ball out of the change cup, press it to the inside rim of the wheel, and flick it. I keep the ball in the corner of my eye as I watch Old Slim lay out checks at a frenzied pace. The ball slows to a certain speed, and I wave my hand over the table, saying, "No more bets." Old Slim, as usual, hastens to get a last few checks on the layout, in defiance of my declaration. It's no problem—he's not watching the wheel. The ball finally succumbs to gravity, and slides down from the inside rim. It dances around—the wheel is still going too fast—and finally settles in the green space, 00. Old Slim curses—he never bets the zeroes. I mark the spot, and sweep the checks off the table. The moment I remove the marker, he's placing checks down at a frenzied pace again. I start mucking checks with my left hand, while I slow the wheel a bit with my right.

Old Slim wins on the next spin, two checks straight up on the number. I push three and a half stacks out to him, and he tosses a few checks towards me across the layout. A tip. I take the checks, knock them loudly on the edge of the wheel, and set them down in a specific place on the rim. Over the next few spins, he keeps "winning," but he puts so many checks out on the table, that he usually gets back less than he bet for the hand. The House [casino] loves players like him.

All too soon, he runs out of checks, and walks off grumbling. I muck up the last of his checks, straighten up the stacks, and fish the ball out of the wheel. Then I look at the checks he toked me, and break them down. Twelve checks, three dollars. I place three silver checks (the ones that are worth something) alongside them, and call out, "Check change three." The Assistant Pit Boss calls out confirmation without looking over, and I drop the three checks in my shirt pocket. Then I take the Roulette checks down off the wheel, and add them to the stacks, and start waiting again.

Blackjack dealers have to deal with all types of people, both good and bad, during their shifts. © Nik Wheeler/Corbis.

Obnoxious Customers

Ten or fifteen minutes later, three tourists walk up. They're young, arrogant college kids, like so many I've seen before. They each toss a Twenty out onto the table. I ask their preference, and they tell me that they want One Dollar checks. I take one check from each of three colors, and stack them on the rim of the wheel, and put a "20" marker on top of the stack. I change up their money for checks, one stack each, and they start playing. After four spins, one of them is already out of checks. He tosses another Twenty out, but before I can change it up, I feel a tap on my shoulder. I clap out, clear my hands, and step to the side. One of the other dealers, Jeff, takes my place. Jeff has a magic touch on the Roulette wheel. He'll string along tipping customers for long periods of time, squeezing tips out of them without letting them actually win much. As far as I know, it's just luck and a charming personality, but it seems like he almost always comes out with more money than any of the players at his table. But that's not too surprising, really . . . ninety percent of the players at Roulette walk away losers, anyway. I drop the three dollars into the Toke Box on my way out of the Pit. Amusingly enough, though, if you ask 100 gamblers how they're doing, 95 of them will tell you that they're "even, or a little ahead." It would be funny if it weren't so pathetic.

Another break, and I'm back in the pit. This time, I'm assigned to an active Blackjack table. I run off my usual line of patter, and chat lightly with the customers. Never anything serious—that might distract me from the job. My rule, not the House's. Once, early on, I was drawn into a heated political argument by a player, and had to be pulled from the table. The Pit Boss hates doing that. So, I watch myself, and try to avoid making any comments that a customer might take offense at.

The hour flies by when I'm actively dealing, especially to friendly players. When I'm tapped out, the Assistant Pit Boss is waiting by the Toke Box. She holds out a slip of paper to me. It's a lunch voucher, a sign that it's lunch time. I drop thirty dollars in tokes into the box—an excellent pull for an hour's work. I walk off to the lunch room in a good mood.

I spend my half hour lunch leisurely eating, and chatting with other employees. This is the only time we can socialize with anyone besides the other dealers, and I like to take advantage of that. That waitress is having her lunch too, so I chat her up a little. She lets me know gently that she's not interested, so I keep it polite. The lunch itself is up to its usual standard—nothing fancy, but definitely a cut above anything I'd fix for myself. I end up spending the last ten minutes of my break in the Break Room, reading a little more.

Problem Customers

When I go back in, I can feel some tension in the air. One of the players at Table 3 is drunk—it's only 1:30, but this isn't surprising—and playing badly. Of course, I get assigned to

Table 3. I run off the patter again, and start dealing. This guy's not just bad, he's an idiot. Of course, the alcohol might have something to do with that. He's so obnoxious, he's scaring other players away to different tables. I keep any hint of my thoughts off my face, and just deal. Eventually, I bust him out, and he wanders off to do god-knows-what.

I end my stand, take my break, and come back in. This time, I'm assigned to Let It Ride, one of the side-action games. There are a couple of older tourists playing, and they seem to be doing well. I wish them luck, and start dealing. They are on a roll . . . holding their own, mostly, with the occasional big win. By the time my hour's up, I have a heavy pocket, and they have more money than when I came. They cheerfully thank me, and I go on my way, dropping the money in the Toke Box on my way out. I've definitely earned my keep today . . . some days, I don't put anything into the Toke Box. That's why tokes are split, though . . . some tables pull in the tokes, some don't, and it would be unfair to the dealers who get stuck at dead tables not to split.

After my break, I get put back on Blackjack again. The drunk guy is back, and still doing badly. He's getting angry about losing, too, which isn't something I want to deal with. But nobody asked me, so I do my job. By now, though, the Assistant Pit Boss is watching over the table. Her presence seems to keep him from exploding, for which I'm grateful. Eventually, though, it gets to be too much for him. After busting him three hands in a row, I beat his 21 with a natural Blackjack. He throws his cards at me, hitting me in the face with them. One of them falls off the table. I calmly collect the cards still on the table, and call out, "Card down inside." It's totally unnecessary, since the Assistant Pit Boss is standing next to me, and already bending down to pick up the card, but it's protocol, and I have to follow it. She puts the card in the rack after checking that it wasn't damaged, and warns the drunk about his behavior. The game continues. After several more hands, I finally bust out the drunk again, and he leaves. I'm glad. . . . I don't like having angry people at my table. One of the other dealers had a guy take a swing at him once. It's not common, but it does happen. And the worst part is that we're not allowed to defend ourselves. That's Security's job.

Finishing Up for the Day

Having no more players at my table, I spread the cards on the table in two sweeping arcs. It looks smooth—it's a very practiced move. After a while, a player comes up and sits down at my table. Time to play again! I scoop up the cards and shuffle. Before I'm done shuffling, I get tapped. Since this table is a shoe (A device that holds multiple decks, usually 6 or 8), not single or double deck, I finish the shuffle, and leave him with a clean shoe.

The day's almost over! A 15-minute break, then another half-hour on, and I'm done! Some of the Swing Shift dealers are already here, so I play a few hands of tonk with them before I go back in. I get put on Roulette again, which is dead. I give the wheel a good spin, and relax. This time, I'm not running tables in my head. . . . The day's almost over, and I'm thinking about going home. I wink at one of the waitresses as she walks by, and she favors me with a smile. But I know she's married . . . it's just a friendly gesture. . . .

I get tapped out by one of the dealers from Swing. He's a new guy that I don't know. I wish him luck, and head back up to the Break Room. I collect my jacket, and head out to the bus stop. About half of the dealers head to one of the neighboring casinos to drink or gamble some before they head home. We're not allowed to patronize the casino we work for. But I don't drink, and being a dealer takes care of most of the gambling urge that I used to have, so I just head home.

It's not a great life, but there are far worse, and I enjoy it. How many people can say that?

The Dark Side of Casinos

Kim K.

For their book Gig: Americans Talk About Their Jobs, *editors John Bowe, Marisa Bowe, Sabin Streeter, Daron Murphy, and Rose Kernochan interviewed people around the country about their work lives. One of the people they interviewed was Kim K., a surveillance officer in a large casino. In the following selection, Kim K. describes her job watching the video monitors of the nine hundred hidden cameras in the casino.*

Kim K. says that her job is to record what she sees on the monitors and to report suspicious activities to security. After three years on the job, she has seen a baccarat dealer flipping hundred-dollar chips into her pocket, gamblers so involved that they do not leave the table to go to the restroom, and customers stealing chips from their table mates.

I'm a surveillance officer at a large casino. My job is I sit in a dark room watching video monitors with about twenty other people. We call up different camera angles, look for any irregularities in procedure, look for any criminal activity, wait for phone calls from the pits—people wanting reviews of things that have taken place on the floor. There's tape rolling all the time. So if somebody raises a stink about anything, we can review it very quickly. And if something's wrong, surveillance can watch closely without the person knowing, and we can record the evidence.

There are nine hundred cameras in this casino. On my keyboard, there's a number pad, and you memorize the number of every camera, so when you want a specific view, you call it up on your monitor. The whole system is state of the art, totally. These cameras—we can zoom in on anything. I mean, the chips, your fingernails, anything. We can see it all in sharp focus.

We're watching the employees and the patrons. I couldn't say which is more likely to do something. It's pretty much fifty-fifty. We've caught tons of patrons engaged in their scams, some hardened criminals, some grandma-types. We've caught dealers doing all kinds of things. There was this young woman recently, a baccarat dealer, she'd taken one of the pockets of her tux jacket—which are normally sewn shut by the wardrobe department—and she'd opened it up. And the top of the pocket came right up to the top of the table. So she was like real suddenly flipping these chips, these hundred-dollar chips, into her pocket. And we caught her.

Our role is to observe, report, and record. That's all we're ever supposed to do. See what's on the tape, relay it to security if that's appropriate, then record it in the log. Not form an opinion.

Being a Blackjack Dealer

It's an okay job. I got into it because I was a blackjack dealer here and I wanted to get off the gaming floor. *That* job was seriously bumming me out. I'd been dealing for I don't know how long—eighteen years, I think—at different places. And I'd just had it. As a dealer, you have to suppress yourself, your feelings. You have to be very, very congenial all the time so the patrons are enjoying themselves. The casino wants dealers who keep the patrons happy, keep them coming back to the tables.

But it's hard to just be congenial all the time. Especially where there's so many people here in trouble—angry people, crazy people—you know, people who can't control themselves in terms of their gambling habit. I mean, you never really know the whole story. You're not at the table with them and then in their bank account with them, and knowing the entire thing. But you can bet that if it's Tuesday night at three A.M., the people at the table have some issues that they're escaping.

You can only kid yourself for so long—it's not helping people. The chances of it bringing them down are much greater. The odds of them losing are really high. Because even if they win, most of these gamblers, because they've got troubles, they're not going to leave the casino while they're up. They want to keep going more and more, so they don't leave until they've lost everything. One of the most common lies about casinos is that we win half the time and lose half the time. That's totally untrue. Because every game has its own odds, and odds are always slightly in favor of the house. Always. Every game at the casino is designed to take your money. And if you play enough, we'll take everything you've got.

A Career Change Needed

There are people who come to this casino—and to every casino—and lose money, and then go straight off and kill themselves. People have killed themselves in the bathroom here. Just this past couple of months, there was a woman who jumped off the bridge near the highway, and a guy who killed himself in the parking lot. Both of them had lost big time. This was driving me—you know, it was really eating at me.

So I went and asked the director of surveillance if there were any possibilities for me in his department. Because I knew what surveillance was all about. I knew I could just basically be alone with the monitors and just be myself. And when the director found out that I had years of gaming knowledge, he got me a job in here pretty quickly.

It's much better than dealing. It's a higher-paying position, I can dress any way I want, joke around, don't have to wear a name tag. Don't have to stand up on my feet all night. And, as a surveillance officer, I work to protect the casino's interests, but I'm not taking anybody's money. I'm even, sometimes, able to give money back to patrons that was mistakenly taken from them. So it just feels a lot better.

And I think I'm pretty good at it. I get good reviews. I'm a truth seeker by nature, so that really helps. I want to know the truth about things. When I look at tape, I'll watch it over and over and over till I am sure I understand what transacted.

Catching Cheaters

Like I just caught some guys cheating on the slot machines. There's been a whole ring of them going around. They're Russians, and we've known they were active, but we couldn't catch them. I found them on the floor and I got all their actions on tape and they were arrested. It was very complicated because they were using shaved coins on the slot machines. And that's a felony, but, well, it's kind of a complicated process to describe—the cheating and how that works—and I'd prefer not to. [Laughs] I think there's probably places on the Internet where you can go and research that on your own. But, they were putting in shaved coins—which are coins that are shaved down so that the slot machine isn't actually registering them—and so they were getting out more than they were putting in. Getting out money without risking anything.

Now, shaved coins come up all the time in slot machines. They're very common. But the object is to actually see a person using them and get security and the police to them while they're on that machine. Catch them in the act. That's pretty tough to coordinate. I was just looking around the casino, because we knew that they were active in Atlantic City and Connecticut. And I ended up watching this particular pair of gentlemen and I saw this behavior that we're told to look for—which is sorting the shaved coins in their hands. That's a telltale giveaway of what they're up to. They take the shaved coins out of the real winnings.

So I noticed it, and then, with something like that, everybody in the room gets involved. Everybody starts following these guys. We all pull up different cameras to make sure we have coverage. I kept the lead cameras on the guys, got in tight and watched them sorting out their coins, while other people got wide shots and followed them from machine to machine. Then, at the same time, my supervisor alerted security and the state police and the gaming commission to what's going on. Because they have to review tape before any action is taken to be absolutely sure. Sometimes it takes too long and we lose people—they've already left—and maybe we get them later, maybe not. The thrill is getting the person arrested on the floor in front of everyone. And with these guys, we did that, we nailed them.

It was very exciting. Definitely. But it was a rarity. There are nights you don't see anything. Lots of times, we just sit there and laugh at the fat people, the bad hairdos, the weirdo stuff. People are pretty funny when they don't know they're being watched. And if we catch something really funny, we'll rewind the tape and watch it over and over. It gets funnier sometimes.

Gamblers Are Just Weird

I've seen all kinds of things—patrons stealing from each other, grabbing handfuls of five-dollar tokens from their neighbors. I've seen men peeing in glasses at the craps tables. They can't, like, leave the game, so they just pee in their beer glass at the table. And it gets weirder—I've seen men playing with themselves at tables. Seen women playing their men at slot machines. Saw men playing with their women's breasts at blackjack tables. Saw two employees having sex in one of the restaurant areas. Seen tons of people fighting, Jerry Springer–like brawls. Like between two women and a guy. Like out-of-control kinds of stuff.

Gamblers are just weird, you know? And some of them are beyond weird. There was a guy last Christmas—I'll never forget this—who we thought might have been a pickpocket but who turned out to be cutting women's hair at the slot machines. It was a very busy night and he was wandering in and out between the aisles. And that's suspicious behavior, so the police on the floor noticed it and called us, so we started watching him and we thought he was pickpocketing. But then the officer who was the lead on this particular watch all of sudden went, "Oh my God! He's not pickpocketing. Look!" And we zoomed in and saw these tiny scissors that he had cupped in his hand. And he's walking up behind these women with long hair and snipping away while they're playing the machines. And he's not saving the hair at all. Just letting it fall. Then he'd walk away and try and find somebody else.

That actually really scared me. Because it was so creepy and he was, like, coming up to these women and we knew he was there. We're screaming at the monitors—obviously these women were never going to hear us. But we kept saying like, "Turn around! Turn around!" And they were far away in another part of the building. But we were screaming and screaming. I was really freaked out. Just because of the creep factor.

The guy, he was arrested and cuffed on the floor and they brought him back to the police and they fingerprinted him and booked him. I don't remember what he was charged with, actually. [Laughs] But he was a high roller. He had like thousand-dollar chips in his pocket, and was wearing a wig and was in disguise because he didn't want anybody to notice him.

After the state police brought him in, they were taking him down to wash the fingerprint ink off his hands. And this is weird, but I was like, all of a sudden, I was like, "I gotta have a real look at him." So I walked out into the hallway and I looked straight at him. It was a very weird moment. You know, it was kind of like, "I know what you just did" kind of thing. But I couldn't really professionally say anything, and I didn't quite know how to look at him. So it was kind of meaningless, but then when I got back into the surveillance room—we have a tape running and a camera running constantly outside that hallway—and I got in the room and rewound the tape and watched the transaction between me and this guy on tape. Just to see myself and—I don't know. I don't know why I did that. Just it was creepy, I guess.

Feeling Burned Out

I've been in surveillance for the last three years. I'm starting to feel a little burned out. It's much better than being a dealer, but it's still the thing, you know? The world. I just don't feel very good about these people, the gamblers. You're seeing human beings at their worst. You're not seeing anything uplifting throughout the day, you know? Very few acts of kindness.

It's just not a good place for me. I don't like casinos. I guess I should just admit that to myself and move on. I never, ever go into a casino when I'm not working. I never gamble. I never have gambled, never will gamble. I got into the business when I was very young. I wasn't even of age to gamble when I started working, so I didn't, and I've just stayed away. That was the smartest decision I ever made. It's a sickness, that's all it is.

I wish I'd done something else with my life. I would have preferred to be in another business, almost any other business, but I've been doing this for so long. I'm almost forty. I don't see how I can change now. [Laughs] I don't know. Maybe I just need a vacation, you know, get out on the beach. See some daylight.

Interview with a Blackjack Dealer

Sandy, interviewed by Robert Romano

In the following selection, Robert Romano interviews "Sandy" (not her real name) about her thirty years working in casinos. Sandy, a middle-aged grandmother of three, started out in 1972 working as a shill, a person employed by a casino to pretend to be a player in order to attract customers to a table. She then got a coveted job dealing blackjack and has been a dealer for over twenty years. Sandy notes that when she started out, dealing cards in a casino was a way to make a good living. However, corporate ownership of casinos and crackdowns by the Internal Revenue Service on "tokes," or tips, have made it more difficult for dealers to make a good living. Sandy also states that she feels she has not accomplished anything by working in casinos.

Robert Romano is a longtime resident of Las Vegas who writes about the city and its culture for the Web site www.about-.com. He has worked in the gaming industry for more than twenty-five years.

Everyone that comes to Las Vegas to live or as a tourist wonders what it would be like to be a dealer. The following is an interview by your site guide of a single parent of two and grandmother of three, an attractive lady in her late forties, that we will call Sandy, a Las Vegas Blackjack dealer.

Guide: How did you get into the casino business?

Sandy: Actually, I started out as a front desk clerk in the Westward Ho. When I turned twenty-one, I got a job as a baccarat shill in the Sands. I went from making $90.00 a week in wages to \$500.00 a week in tokes [tips] and \$1.60 an hour in pay. Being a shill has to be the easiest job I ever had. You just play the game with the house's money until enough real players come to the table, then you take a break until the table needs you again. I could see that the dealers were making the really big bucks though.

I decided then, that I wanted to deal. There was only one female dealer in the blackjack pits when I started to shill in 1972, a black woman. When I decided to do it in 1980, women were starting to deal in all of the casinos.

Guide: You've been dealing for twenty years, then. Where?

Sandy: All over. You see, you keep switching to get a better job. Money wise, that is. Tokes. I started out Downtown at the Mint. In those days you worked Downtown for three to five years before you could even get to the Strip. Now, you can do it in a year and a half. I then did the Fremont, the Silver Dollar, a country and western place that used to be on Boulder Highway, the Westward Ho again, the Union Plaza, the Maxim and the Rio.

Guide: What games?

Sandy: Just Blackjack and Pai Gao. I would say that Blackjack and Roulette are basic to moving up. I know. It doesn't speak well of my ambition that I don't deal Roulette, but I've always been fast at Blackjack, so I moved up some, but not to the jobs at Caesar's, Paris or Bellagio, that kind of place.

Guide: What kind of money did you make in those years?

Sandy: Well, Downtown I made about thirty thousand a year, forty to fifty on the Strip. Bellagio is about fifty to sixty thousand and Caesar's, which has always been the best, about eighty thousand. But you buy a job there or you have to know somebody. You know, juice. The wages to deal in almost all of these places is little more than minimum wage. You make your money in tokes.

Guide: Dealers were most envied for their money back before the IRS cracked down on their tokes. How does the IRS handle the toke situation?

Sandy: Before the middle '80s, it was fine. We were taxed on our wages, which were damned near nothing, while we picked up our tokes in cash in an envelope every day. Depending on what you felt the IRS should get, you declared so much for tokes and paid taxes accordingly. After the IRS got on to us, each casino had to set up a toke committee that would split the tokes and report the daily envelope amount to the IRS every two weeks. The payroll office would use your whole pay check to pay taxes and you would be informed whether you needed to pay more taxes for the period or not. If you needed to pay, you worked payment out with payroll. Now, most places have gone to giving you your tokes every two weeks as part of your paycheck. The taxes are already taken out. I don't like it. Don't know anybody that does.

Guide: Would you join a union?

Sandy: I would, and so would most dealers that I know. You see, things have really changed, money wise for dealers, because things have changed in the casinos. What I mean is, in the old days, the houses were owned by people that made money for themselves and their families. You know, strong individuals. They 'gave the house away' to attract the high roller and keep them. The players toked the dealer, and the dealer spent the money. Now, the corporations own the joints. They feel that the toke that you get is *their* money. Money that you shouldn't be taking from them. The IRS gets their part of all of your wages and all of your tokes, and the wages are minimum. This is a right to work state. I've been told that I was laid off by phone, with no explanation given. They can do that. For example; before, many of the places had retirement plans. Now they got 401Ks. With a union we could go for higher wages and try to get back some of the esteem that we used to have. I don't think that you'll see the dealers organized in the near future, though. The houses don't want to see it.

Guide: How much of a kick do you get out of 'beating' customers?

Sandy: None at all! Only the idiots get a kick out of beating customers. Customers are our bread and butter. They're tokes! You want them to win. Oh, now and then, I love sticking it to some customers. Some get pretty damned obnoxious, you know. I have a dealer friend who once had a male customer pee on her feet. Yes! Right under the table. Peed on her feet while she was dealing. Think she minded beating him? They threw him out after the peeing thing though. I once had one that picked his nose and wiped his finger on the cards where I could see what he was putting there. I had enjoyed beating him because of the language that he was using towards me before that. He was told to take his business elsewhere. I had one lady who always lost, no matter who dealt to her.

Her husband used to sit on a stool nearby to watch her play. He didn't play. She once put up a nickel for herself ($5.00 bet) and a quarter for me ($25.00 bet). Then she said to me, "I hope you lose it, b—." Can you imagine if I liked beating her or not? Then it's not like I'm beating anyone. I have to play by the book, and I can't manipulate the cards in a shoe. So the rules are beating you along with your own way of playing the game. It's not me. I've had people flip their cards at me like Frisbees. They lose their money, then want to take it out on the dealer. Being cursed at is very common.

Guide: How often do you catch customers trying to cheat?

Sandy: With shoe play, it's rare anymore that anyone is caught cheating. I'm paying attention to the play of the customer, and so is the floorman and the surveillance cameras up above.

It's hard for a customer to cheat anymore. Marking cards and card counting used to be the most popular methods, but there is little, if any, single deck blackjack around anymore for the normal customer. You're more likely to find a dealer trying to steal these days. Why, I guess because as long as you're dealing with money, someone will be around who tries to steal it. Mind you, there is less stealing by dealers then there used to be. The security cameras took care of that. These days they are all over the place, and most of the action is recorded on tape. It's not worth the black check that you 'might' get away with.

Guide: How much do you enjoy dealing?

Sandy: To be honest with you, I don't enjoy it. I haven't 'enjoyed' it for years. Oh, I loved it once. It was good money, and it was fun. Then, the corporations moved in, the IRS moved in, the dealers ceased to be a close knit group, and my feet and hands started to feel bad. It got boring. Right now, my hands can barely hold a deck of cards. Here I am twenty years later, and I don't feel like I accomplished anything. That is my biggest gripe. I wouldn't recommend it other than as an easy way to make good money.

Guide: Is it time to become a floorperson?

If my hands get worse, that's what I will have to do. I'll tell them that I'm interested in training for floor, and hopefully they'll let me. I'll have to learn a couple more games, but I can handle that. Although, I don't know if I can handle the responsibility. You have to watch four to six tables, rate customers, and a lot more. The thing that scares me most is getting into the rat race of competition to move up in the casino management line. What will I turn into? I've seen too many dealers go to the floor and become Gestapo-like animals. I don't want to be like that, but I can understand where it might be necessary to move up. My hands will let me know what I have to do. My hands are the whole job.

Organizations to Contact

American Gaming Association (AGA)
555 13th St. NW, Ste. 1010 East
   Washington, DC   20004-1109
(202) 637-6500 • fax: (202) 637-6507
e-mail: info@americangaming.org
Web site: www.americangaming.org

AGA represents the gaming-entertainment industry by addressing regulatory, legislative, and educational issues. The association serves as a clearinghouse for information, develops aggressive educational and advocacy programs, and provides leadership in addressing industry issues that are of public concern, such as problems with underage gambling. AGA publishes the newsletter *Inside the AGA*.

Gam-Anon International Service Office
PO Box 157, Whitestone, NY   11357
(718) 352-1671 • fax: (718) 746-2571
e-mail: gamanonoffice1@aol.com
Web site: www.gam-anon.org

Gam-Anon describes its mission as being "here to assist you in resolving the problems you are facing in your life due to the gambling problem." It has literature about compulsive gambling and how to cope with the crises that often accompany the syndrome.

Gamblers Anonymous (GA)
PO Box 17173, Los Angeles, CA   90017
(213) 386-8789 • fax: (213) 386-0030
e-mail: isomain@gamblersanonymous.org
Web site: www.gamblersanonymous.org

GA is an organization of compulsive gamblers who seek to stop gambling and to help other compulsive gamblers do the same. It publishes pamphlets on compulsive gambling, a list of local Gamblers Anonymous meetings, and the monthly *Lifelines Bulletin*.

Institute for the Study of Gambling and Commercial Gaming
College of Business Administration
  University of Nevada, Reno, NV   89957
(702) 784-1442 • fax: (702) 784-1057
Web site: www.unr.edu/gaming/index.asp

The institute offers courses and degrees in management and other areas of gambling. It holds national and international conferences on gambling. The institute publishes books and reports on current issues and trends in legalized gambling and copublishes, with the National Council on Problem Gambling, the quarterly *Journal of Gambling Studies*.

National Coalition Against Legalized Gambling (NCALG)
100 Maryland Ave. NE, Rm. 311, Washington, DC   20002
(800) 664-2680
e-mail: ncalg@ncalg.org
Web site: www.ncalg.org

NCALG opposes the gaming industry and fights for federal laws curtailing gambling. It also provides research, technical, and fund-raising support to grassroots groups opposing the expansion of gambling in their states. NCALG publishes a quarterly newsletter.

National Congress of American Indians (NCAI)
1301 Connecticut Ave. NW, Ste. 200, Washington, DC   20036
(202) 466-7767 • fax: (202) 466-7797
e-mail: ncai@ncai.org
Web site: www.ncai.org

NCAI is a tribal organization that represents 600,000 American Indians who seek to protect, conserve, and develop their natural and human resources. NCAI believes that gaming is a right of American Indian tribes and an aspect of tribal sovereignty. It asserts that the 1988 Indian Gaming Regulatory Act was a concession to the state and federal governments and that further concessions are unwarranted. NCAI publishes a quarterly newsletter, the *Sentinel.*

National Council on Problem Gambling
216 G St. NE, Ste. 200, Washington, DC   20002
(800) 522-4700 • fax: (212) 547-9206
e-mail: ncpg@ncpgambling.org
Web site: www.ncpgambling.org

The council includes health, education, and law professionals, recovering gamblers, and others concerned with compulsive gambling. It conducts seminars and training programs on the identification and treatment of compulsive gambling behavior. The council publishes books, brochures, videos, the quarterly *National Council on Problem Gambling Newsletter,* and the quarterly *Journal of Gambling Studies,* which explores the psychological behavior of both controlled and pathological gamblers.

National Indian Gaming Association (NIGA)
224 Second St. SE, Washington, DC   20003
(202) 546-7711 • fax: (202) 546-1755
e-mail: estevens@indiangaming.org
Web site: www.indiangaming.org

NIGA comprises American Indian tribes that operate bingo games or gambling casinos. It works for the successful operation of Indian casinos as well as effective tribal, state, and federal regulation. NIGA publishes the quarterly newsletter *Moccasin Telegraph.*

North American Association of State and Provincial Lotteries (NASPL)
2775 Bishop Rd., Ste. B, Willoughby Hills, OH   44092
(216) 241-2310 • fax: (216) 241-4350

e-mail: nasplhq@aol.com
Web site: www.naspl.org

The mission of NASPL is to assemble and disseminate information about the benefits of state and provincial lottery organizations. It also works to maintain public confidence and support for state and provincial-sponsored lottery organizations, believing that these lotteries are important means of generating revenue to meet public needs. NASPL publishes *Lottery Insights* monthly.

Public Gaming Research Institute (PGRI)
218 Main St., #203, Kirkland, WA   98033
(425) 985-3159 • fax: (206) 232-2564
e-mail: raquelpgr2@aol.com
Web site: www.publicgaming.org

PGRI studies various issues concerning the gaming industry, including legislation and marketing. It publishes the monthly magazines *Indian Gaming* and *Public Gaming International*, the latter devoted entirely to North American and international lotteries.

Responsible Gaming Council (RGC)
3080 Yonge St., Ste. 4070, Box 90
    Toronto, ON   M4N 3N1
    Canada
(416) 499-9800 • fax: (416) 499-8260
e-mail: cfcg@interlog.com
Web site: www.cfcg.org

The RGC is a nonprofit organization that works with individuals and communities to address gambling in a healthy and responsible way. The council undertakes research and public awareness programs designed to prevent gambling-related problems.

For Further Research

Books

H. Lee Barnes, *Dummy Up and Deal: Inside the Culture of Casino Dealing*. Reno: University of Nevada Press, 2002.

Steven and Frederick Barthelme, *Double Down: The Gripping Account of a Two-Year Gambling Splurge and Its Aftermath*. Orlando, FL: Harcourt, 1999.

Andy Bellin, *Poker Nation*. New York: Perennial, 2002.

Linda Berman and Mary-Ellen Seigal, *Behind the 8-Ball: A Recovery Guide for the Families of Gamblers*. Lincoln, NE: iUniverse, 2000.

Lyle Berman with Marvin Karlins, *I'm All In! High Stakes, Big Business and the Birth of the World Poker Tour*. New York: Cardoza, 2005.

Don Catlin, *The Lottery Book: The Truth Behind the Numbers*. Chicago: Bonus, 2003.

John Chin, *A Way to Quit (For Problem Gamblers)*. Cincinnati: Writer's Digest, 2000.

Michael Craig, *The Professor, the Banker and the Suicide King: Inside the Richest Poker Game of All Time*. New York: Warner, 2005.

Kim Isaac Eisler, *Revenge of the Pequots: How a Small Native American Tribe Created the World's Most Profitable Casino*. Lincoln: University of Nebraska Press, 2002.

Earl L. Grinols, *Gambling in America: Costs and Benefits*. Cambridge: Cambridge University Press, 2004.

Gregory L. Jantz, *Turning the Tables on Gambling*. Colorado Springs, CO: Shaw, 2001.

David Kushner, *Jonny Magic and the Card Shark Kids: How a Gang of Geeks Beat the Odds and Stormed Las Vegas.* New York: Random House, 2005.

Jackson Lears, *Something for Nothing: Luck in America.* New York: Penguin, 2003.

Bill Lee, *Born to Lose: Memoirs of a Compulsive Gambler.* Center City, MN: Hazelden, 2005.

Steven Andrew Light and Kathryn R.L. Rand, *Indian Gaming and Tribal Sovereignty: The Casino Compromise.* Lawrence: University Press of Kansas, 2005.

Paul Lyons, ed., *The Greatest Gambling Stories Ever Told: Thirty-One Tales of Risk and Reward.* Guilford, CT: Lyons, 2002.

James McManus, *Positively Fifth Street.* New York: Picador, 2003.

Ben Mezrich, *Bringing Down the House: The Inside Story of Six MIT Students Who Took Las Vegas for Millions.* New York: Free Press, 2002.

Chad Millman, *The Odds: One Season, Three Gamblers and the Death of Their Las Vegas.* Cambridge, MA: Da Capo, 2002.

Robert R. Perkinson, *The Gambling Addiction Patient Workbook.* Thousand Oaks, CA: Sage, 2003.

William Poundstone, *The Untold Story of the Scientific Betting System That Beat the Casinos and Wall Street.* New York: Hill and Wang, 2005.

Gerda Rieth, ed., *Gambling: Who Wins? Who Loses?* Amherst, NY: Prometheus, 2003.

Gary Stephen Ross, *Stung: The Incredible Obsession of Brian Molony.* Toronto: McClelland and Steward, 2002.

Jean Scott with Angela Sparks, *More Frugal Gambling*. Las Vegas: Huntington, 2003.

The Tiltboys, *Tales from the Tiltboys*, ed. Kim Scheinberg. Champaign, IL: Sports Publishing, 2005.

Periodicals

Robert Ankeny, "Casinos Bring Tax Money, Jobs, but Concerns Remain," *Crain's Detroit Business*, November 25, 2002.

Jonathan Blum, "From Gambling to Grief," *Scholastic Action*, February 7, 2005.

Matt Bradley, "Campuses Slow to Deal with Growth in Gambling," *Christian Science Monitor*, January 25, 2005.

Campus Life "What's with My Life?" January/February, 2005.

Marc Cooper, "Sit and Spin," *Atlantic*, December 2005.

Kathleen Fackelmann, "Seniors Could Be Easy Gambling Prey," *USA Today*, January 19, 2005.

Peter Gumbel, Massimo Calabresi, Viveca Novak, Coco Masters, and Jeanne McDowell, "How the U.S. Is Getting Beat in Online Gambling," *Time Canada*, November 28, 2005.

Jeffery Kluger, Melissa August, Helen Gibson, Noah Isackson, Coco Masters, and Jeffery Ressner, "When Gambling Becomes Obsessive," *Time*, August 1, 2005.

Alison Knopt, "High Rate of Gambling Problems Found in Substance Abuse Counselors," *Alcoholism & Drug Abuse Weekly*, April 25, 2005.

Wendy Koch, "It's Always Poker Night on Campus," *USA Today*, December 23, 2005.

Barry Koltnow, "Casino Marathon: A Three-Day Streak Across the Southern California Indian Gambling Landscape," *Orange County Register*, May 1, 2005.

G. Jeffrey MacDonald, "Will Teens Know When to Fold in the Popular Poker Craze?" *Christian Science Monitor*, December 22, 2004.

Alexandra Marks, "Just a Coincidence? Bankruptcies Highest Where Casinos Are," *Christian Science Monitor*, March 19, 2004.

Tim McGirk, "A Cabbie's Luck," *Time*, December 26, 2005.

People, "I Won $1 Million—Twice!" June 27, 2005.

Cheryl Petten, "Women Gamble with Their Lives," *Alberta Sweetgrass* (Canada), November 2003.

Dan Seligman, "In Defense of Gambling," *Forbes*, June 23, 2003.

Brad Stone, "Going All In for Online Poker," *Newsweek*, August 15, 2005.

Marianne Szegedy-Maszak, "The Worst of All Bets," *U.S. News & World Report*, May 23, 2005.

Alex Tresniowski, Richard Jerome, Vickie Bane, Stacey Wilson, Jeff Hanson, and Ruth Laney, "Goldrush," *People*, November 21, 2005.

Mark Walsh and Dan Beucke, "You Can Bet—but Don't Call It Gambling," *Business Week*, September 19, 2005.

Tom Weir, "Online Sports Betting Spins Out of Control," *USA Today*, August 22, 2003.

Kelly Whiteside, "NCAA Official: We Do Have a Gambling Problem on Our Campuses," *USA Today*, June 6, 2003.

George F. Will, "Electronic Morphine," *Newsweek*, November 25, 2002.

Internet Sources

Kathy Bassett, "Kathy's Story: Presentation to Voices of the Heartland," Oklahoma Association for Gambling Addiction Awareness, July 25, 2005. www.oagaa.org/html/body_kathy_s_story.html.

Amy Green, "Profile: Pastor John Eades Shares Own Struggle with Gambling," *United Methodist News Service*, October 8, 2002. www.wfn.org/2002.10/msg00092.html.

Ronald "Buzz" Gutierrez, "Revenue Sharing and Reservation Shopping Create Greed," *Indian Country Today*, 2005. www.indiancountry.com/content.cf?id=1096411998.

Janet Campbell Hale, "Letter From Hell: Confessions of a Native American Gambler," *Electron Press*, 2005. www.electronpress.com/magazine/5/GAMBLING_ESSAY.htm.

Jekyll, "I Won the Lottery!" *Transcendental Floss*, 2005. www.transcendentalfloss.com/2005/05/i-won-the-lottery.html.

Nancy Steele, "On the Job: A Change Attendant," Jobmonkey.com. www.jobmonkey.com/casino/html/on_the_job_change.html.

Index

acting, poker and, 37–38
Addison, Steve, 40, 41
Affleck, Ben, 36–37
amateur gamblers
    celebrity poker players, 31–38
    high rollers, 24–25
    lower rollers, 21–30
American Gaming Association
  (AGA), 96
antidepressants, 13
Arieh, Josh, 15

Beacon, Eric, 42–43
blackjack, 28
blackjack dealers, 75–82, 84–85,
  90–96
blame, 62

card clubs, underground, 39–44
card counting, 28
card dealers, 75–82, 84–85, 90–96
card games, 23–24
Caselli, Michael, 31
casinos
    cheaters in, 86–87, 93–94
    comps given out by, 24–30,
      29–30
    problem customers in, 79–82,
      93
    spread of, 10
    surveillance in, 83–89
    working at
      as blackjack dealer, 84–85,
        90–96
      as surveillance officer,
        83–89
      typical day of, 75–82
celebrity poker players, 31–38
comps, given out by casinos,
  24–30
compulsive gamblers

belief system of, 61
experiences of, 51–67
family member experience of,
  68–73
lies by, 59–60
online gambling and, 10–11
profile of, 11–12
questions to identify, 55
rise in number of, 10
suicide by, 68–69, 73
see also gambling addiction
crime, gambling addiction and,
  57–58, 72

deuces wild video poker, 28–29
discipline, 32
DuVall, Jason, 75

faith, in luck, 60–61
Forman, Dana, 59, 60, 61, 62, 63

Gam-Anon International Service
  Office, 96
gamblers
    belief system of, 61
    celebrity poker players, 31–38
    high rollers, 24–25
    low rollers, 21–30
    professional, 13–20
    see also compulsive gamblers
Gamblers Anonymous, 13, 60,
  96–97
gambling
    legalized, 10
    online, 10–11, 31–36, 46–50
    popularity of, 10
    rush from, 58–59
    underage, 11–12, 41
gambling addiction
    attempt to cover up, 61–62

coping with, 12–13
crime and, 57–58, 72
growth of, 10, 11–12
to lottery tickets, 51–63
online gambling and, 10–11, 46–50
path to, 55–57
reasons for, 60
see also compulsive gamblers
Gamblock software, 49
Giuliani, Rudy, 42
government, legalized gambling and, 10, 53–54

Harding, Lisa, 11
high rollers, 24–25
Hollywood, poker craze in, 35–36
HollywoodPoker.com, 35–36
Howard, Toni, 36–37

Institute for the Study of Gambling and Commercial Gambling, 97
Internet gambling. *See* online gambling

Kim, Alice II., 39

Laak, Phil, 41
Las Vegas, 10, 25–26
see also casinos
legalized gambling, 10
lies, by gamblers, 59–60
Lipscomb, Steve, 18
losing streaks, 58–59
lotteries, state-run, 10
lottery tickets, addiction to, 51–63
low rollers, experience of, 21–30
luck, 60–61

magical thinking, 60
Mayfair, 42–43
money, lost to gambling, 63
Moneymaker, Chris, 18, 37, 40

National Coalition Against Legalized Gambling, 97
National Congress of American Indians, 97–98
National Council on Problem Gambling, 11, 13, 98
National Indian Gaming Association, 98
New York City, underground poker clubs in, 39–44
Nibert, David, 53, 57–58
No Limit Texas Hold'em, 42
North American Association of State and Provincial Lotteries, 98–99

online gambling
addiction to, 46–50
poker, 11, 31–36
rise of, 10–11

Paton, Maureen, 46
poker
acting and, 37–38
Hollywood craze for, 35–36
online, 11, 31–36
online *vs.* live, 32–35
popularity of, 16–20
underground poker clubs, 39–44
poker players
celebrity, 31–38
life of professional, 13–20
underground, 39–44
poker tournaments, 16–17
poker world, changes in, 17–18

professional gamblers, 13–20
Public Gaming Research Institute, 99

Raymer, Greg, 19
religion, 60
religious organizations, gambling sponsored by, 10
residential treatment programs, 66–67
Responsible Gaming Council, 99
Romano, Robert, 90

Scott, Jean, 21–30
scratch tickets, addiction to, 51–63
secrecy, 11
Selbst, Vanessa, 11
senior citizens, as problem gamblers, 12
slot clubs, 27
slot machines, 26–29, 34
state lotteries, 10, 53–54
suicide, by gambling addicts, 68–69, 73
superstition, 60

surveillance officers, in casinos, 83–89

teenagers, as problem gamblers, 11–12, 41
television coverage, of poker tournaments, 19–20
temptation, 62
Texas Hold'em, 34–35, 42
treatment, for gambling addiction, 13

underage gambling, 11–12, 41
underground poker clubs, 39–44

Vahedi, Amir, 37–38
video poker, 26–29, 34

Whyte, Keith, 12
women, online gambling by, 46
Wong, Michelle, 68
Woods, James, 31–38
World Poker Tour, 17, 19
World Series of Poker Tournament, 16–20
Wright, Chris, 51